Affirmative Action

Other books in the Issues on Trial series

Affirmative Action

Justin Karr, Book Editor

GREENHAVEN PRESS
A part of Gale, Cengage Learning

Detroit • New York • San Francisco • New Haven, Conn • Waterville, Maine • London

GALE
CENGAGE Learning

Christine Nasso, *Publisher*
Elizabeth Des Chenes, *Managing Editor*

For more information, contact:
Greenhaven Press
27500 Drake Rd.
Farmington Hills, MI 48331-3535
Or you can visit our Internet site at gale.cengage.com

LIBRARY OF CONGRESS CATALOGING-IN-PUBLICATION DATA

Affirmative action / Justin Karr, book editor.
       p. cm. -- (Issues on trial)
    Includes bibliographical references and index.
    ISBN-13: 978-0-7377-3854-4 (hardcover)
    ISBN-10: 0-7377-3854-5 (hardcover)
    1. Affirmative action programs--United States. 2. Discrimination--Government policy--United States. 3. Minorities--Government policy--United States. I. Karr, Justin.
    JK766.4.A44 2007
    342.7308'5--dc22
                                                               2007032381

Printed in the United States of America
2 3 4 5 6 7 12 11 10 09 08

Contents

Chapter 2: Housing

Chapter 3: Employment

Chapter 4: College Admissions

Foreword

The U.S. courts have long served as a battleground for the most highly charged and contentious issues of the time. Divisive matters are often brought into the legal system by activists who feel strongly for their cause and demand an official resolution. Indeed, subjects that give rise to intense emotions or involve closely held religious or moral beliefs lay at the heart of the most polemical court rulings in history. One such case was *Brown v. Board of Education* (1954), which ended racial segregation in schools. Prior to *Brown*, the courts had held that blacks could be forced to use separate facilities as long as these facilities were equal to that of whites.

For years many groups had opposed segregation based on religious, moral, and legal grounds. Educators produced heartfelt testimony that segregated schooling greatly disadvantaged black children. They noted that in comparison to whites, blacks received a substandard education in deplorable conditions. Religious leaders such as Martin Luther King Jr. preached that the harsh treatment of blacks was immoral and unjust. Many involved in civil rights law, such as Thurgood Marshall, called for equal protection of all people under the law, as their study of the Constitution had indicated that segregation was illegal and un-American. Whatever their motivation for ending the practice, and despite the threats they received from segregationists, these ardent activists remained unwavering in their cause.

Those fighting against the integration of schools were mainly white southerners who did not believe that whites and blacks should intermingle. Blacks were subordinate to whites, they maintained, and society had to resist any attempt to break down strict color lines. Some white southerners charged that segregated schooling was *not* hindering blacks' education. For example, Virginia attorney general J. Lindsay Almond asserted, "With the help and the sympathy and the love and respect of the white people of the South, the colored man has risen under that educational process to a place of eminence and respect throughout the nation. It has served him well." So when the Supreme Court ruled against the segregationists in *Brown*, the South responded with vociferous cries of protest. Even government leaders criticized the decision. The governor of Arkansas, Orval Faubus, stated that he would not "be a party to any attempt to force acceptance of change to which the people are so overwhelmingly opposed." Indeed, resistance to integration was so great that when black students arrived at the formerly all-white Central High School in Arkansas, federal troops had to be dispatched to quell a threatening mob of protesters.

Nevertheless, the *Brown* decision was enforced and the South integrated its schools. In this instance, the Court, while not settling the issue to everyone's satisfaction, functioned as an instrument of progress by forcing a major social change. Historian David Halberstam observes that the *Brown* ruling "deprived segregationist practices of their moral legitimacy. . . . It was therefore perhaps the single most important moment of the decade, the moment that separated the old order from the new and helped create the tumultuous era just arriving." Considered one of the most important victories for civil rights, *Brown* paved the way for challenges to racial segregation in many areas, including on public buses and in restaurants.

In examining *Brown*, it becomes apparent that the courts play an influential role—and face an arduous challenge—in shaping the debate over emotionally charged social issues. Judges must balance competing interests, keeping in mind the high stakes and intense emotions on both sides. As exemplified by *Brown*, judicial decisions often upset the status quo and initiate significant changes in society. Greenhaven Press's Issues on Trial series captures the controversy surrounding influential court rulings and explores the social ramifications of such decisions from varying perspectives. Each anthology highlights one social issue—such as the death penalty, students' rights, or wartime civil liberties. Each volume then focuses on key historical and contemporary court cases that helped mold the issue as we know it today. The books include a compendium of primary sources—court rulings, dissents, and immediate reactions to the rulings—as well as secondary sources from experts in the field, people involved in the cases, legal analysts, and other commentators opining on the implications and legacy of the chosen cases. An annotated table of contents, an in-depth introduction, and prefaces that overview each case all provide context as readers delve into the topic at hand. To help students fully probe the subject, each volume contains book and periodical bibliographies, a comprehensive index, and a list of organizations to contact. With these features, the Issues on Trial series offers a well-rounded perspective on the courts' role in framing society's thorniest, most impassioned debates.

Introduction

Affirmative action is an evolving legal and social strategy influenced not only by the executive, legislative, and judicial branches of U.S. government, but also by public opinion. The earliest presidential acts of significance in the movement toward affirmative action include Franklin D. Roosevelt's insistence that all Americans, regardless of gender or race, must be included in the New Deal programs of the 1930s, and Harry S. Truman's integration of the armed forces in the late 1940s. In 1961, President John F. Kennedy prohibited government contractors from racial discrimination by executive order, stating that contractors "take affirmative action to ensure that applicants are employed and that employees are treated during employment, without regard to their race, creed, color, or national origin." Similarly, President Lyndon B. Johnson championed efforts for equal opportunities in employment, education of the poor, and training of the unskilled.

Yet the two most important forces in the applications and limitations of affirmative action stem from the Civil Rights Act of 1964 and the Equal Protection Clause of the Fourteenth Amendment. The Civil Rights Act of 1964 provided the statutory framework for affirmative action in education and employment; it also created the Equal Employment Opportunity Commission. Conversely, the Equal Protection Clause, by declaring that no state shall "deny to any person . . . the equal protection of the laws," defends the rights of individuals while challenging preferential treatment of groups. The result is a balancing act for legislators and jurists between protecting individual rights and advancing social justice for historically disadvantaged groups.

The Supreme Court on Affirmative Action

In *Reed v. Reed* (1971), the Supreme Court ruled that unequal treatment of men and women is unconstitutional, citing the

Equal Protection Clause of the Fourteenth Amendment. This unanimous decision guided court decisions and legislative action not only for affirmative action, but also for other gender-discrimination cases involving maternity leave rules, sexual harassment, and promotion equity.

While affirmative-action programs have not greatly impacted employment of white women, minority women have been helped. Studies suggest, however, that minority women are still underrepresented in a number of areas, such as the legal and medical professions and positions of power in general. It should be noted that the Supreme Court has never specifically ruled on gender-based affirmative-action programs. If and when the Court does rule, the question becomes whether the Court will subject such programs to the same high level of review it applies to racial preferences.

Turning from issues of equality to those of purpose in housing laws, the Supreme Court declared that more than discriminatory results must be shown: Proof of racially discriminatory intent is necessary to prove a violation of the Equal Protection Clause (*Arlington Heights v. Metropolitan*, 1977). Nonetheless, earlier decisions by the Supreme Court have not been subjected to the racist-intent test. Therefore, racially restrictive covenants in housing deeds are invalid; also, racial discrimination, whether public or private, in the sale or rental of property is prohibited. Yet in practice, racism and segregation exist in housing matters. The Court banned racial discrimination then restricted the remedy, affirmative action, by requiring tangible proof of racist intent. While review of affirmative-action programs would in time turn from issues of purpose to levels of scrutiny, much of present-day housing matters are regulated by the Civil Rights Division of the Department of Justice, Housing and Urban Development, and numerous federal programs.

In 1995, the Supreme Court in *Adarand Constructors, Inc. v. Pena* moved from an intermediate level of judicial review to strict scrutiny. The Court reasoned that only a high level of review could determine whether a racial preference was benign and not unduly burdensome to the historically favored race. However, since the government must be permitted to address the lingering effects of racial discrimination, some race-based actions would satisfy strict scrutiny if they served a compelling governmental interest and were narrowly tailored, as opposed to a blanket racial preference.

The Court—specifically Justice Sandra Day O'Connor, who also wrote the decision in *Adarand*—proved affirmative action could withstand strict scrutiny with the ruling in *Grutter v. Bollinger* (2003). Citing the educational and social benefits of diversity as the compelling interest, the Court ruled that the University of Michigan Law School's admission program used race as just one of many factors in making admission decisions. This individualistic approach was deemed narrowly tailored and not unreasonably harmful to white students. The admission program—unlike past admission cases that used quotas, which are unconstitutional, or blanket racial preferences, which may be struck down—used race as a "plus" factor, which avoided branding race as a predominant factor. This holistic method serves as the guide for other universities that seek diversity on campus.

Corrective Goals

Before enactment of the Civil Rights Act of 1964, many businesses and factories discriminated against minorities. After passage of the Act, most companies worked to comply with the law; however, the remnants of past discrimination carried forward. Therefore, courts and legislators found it necessary to strike down racially neutral laws and impose corrective laws, which became known as affirmative action. These laws, in essence, sought to remedy historical discrimination.

While these corrective laws provided increased employment opportunities and enhanced access to college, many have claimed that favoring one group over another is reverse discrimination. Others have argued that affirmative action demeans minorities, sets groups against one another, imposes limits on freedom of choice, and creates bureaucratic excesses. Many suggest that affirmative-action policies will not continue in the long term given the divided opinion of the U.S. population; many Americans feel that affirmative action has done its job and should end. A strong, organized anti-affirmative-action movement has welcomed recent restrictive federal legislative and court decisions, particularly those emphasizing strict scrutiny and color-blind proposals. Still, voluntary affirmative-action programs continue, stressing the continuing need to achieve social justice and equal opportunity.

A different method of promoting social justice uses race-neutral as opposed to race-based remedies. By relying on a standard such as income, race-neutral plans are less likely to stereotype or stir racial resentment. A program designed to help the poverty-stricken would reach all disadvantaged persons of any race. The downside, however, is that the majority of people in any income bracket are white, and thus aid may not reach minorities.

Progressive Goals

In contrast to the corrective, remedial goals of achieving social justice, affirmative action has taken on a new model—progressive, forward-looking plans. The best example of such a non-remedial program is found in the diversity rationale. First championed by Justice Lewis Powell then applied in *Grutter* by Justice O'Connor, diversity plans rely on racial classifications considered necessary to further a compelling interest in the present and future. Diversity will promote learning outcomes, prepare students for a multicultural employment society, and foster superior leadership for those exposed to a dissimilar learning environment. Accordingly, Justice O'Connor stated: "In order to cultivate a set of leaders with legitimacy in the eyes of the citizenry, it is necessary that the path to leadership be visibly open to talented and qualified individuals of every race and ethnicity."

Opponents of affirmative action continue to stress that no racial preference be allowed, citing the rights of the individual under the Equal Protection Clause of the Fourteenth Amendment. Consequently, Justice Anthony Kennedy, a potential swing vote in a number of upcoming cases, favors a color-blind policy. In his *Grutter* dissent, he declared: "Preferment by race, when resorted to by the State, can be the most divisive of all policies, containing within it the potential to destroy confidence in the Constitution and in the idea of equality." Likewise, law professor L. Darnell Weeden has claimed, "[R]ace-based diversity policy promotes notions of racial superiority and racial inferiority."

The Future of Affirmative Action

Despite these protests, the *Grutter* model has encouraged diversity-based admission programs in colleges across the country. In fact, some colleges have extended diversity programs to financial-aid decisions in recent years. School administrators have reasoned that such financial-aid programs help recruit and retain minority students while demonstrating the institution's commitment to diversity. For the Court, the next affirmative-action challenge in education will test whether voluntary diversity programs in secondary education pass both the *Grutter* diversity standard and the Constitution. Correspondingly, both Washington and Kentucky have cases before the Supreme Court that will be decided by 2008. The diversity rationale has also been extended to employment, echoing the Court's declaration in *Grutter* that "the skills needed in today's increasingly global marketplace can only be developed through exposure to widely diverse people, cultures, ideas, and viewpoints."

Even as diversity-fueled progressive programs have mustered momentum, the question remains: Will the new Supreme Court respect the precedence of *Grutter* or will it take an activist, color-blind stance and roll back the gains of affirmative action? The architect of this generation's affirmative action, Justice Sandra Day O'Connor, retired in 2006. Two new conservatives on the Court, Chief Justice John Roberts and Justice Samuel Alito, may rule against racial preferences, both corrective and progressive.

Recently, individual states have altered the scope of affirmative action with proposals prohibiting racial preferences. The first such action was California's Proposition 209 in 1996, which precluded affirmative action in the public sector. Similar initiatives have been passed in Washington and in Michigan, where voters approved a proposal to amend the state constitution, banning affirmative-action programs that give preference to groups or individuals based on race, gender, color, ethnicity, or national origin in public education, contracting, or employment. In Florida, the legislature passed the "One Florida" plan, banning affirmative action in state universities and contracting.

Other states have been targeted for anti-affirmative-action proposals, including Nevada, Arizona, Colorado, Missouri, Nebraska, Oregon, South Dakota, Utah, Wisconsin, and Wyoming. However, to amend the constitution in any state, affirmative action must be a controversial issue (in Nevada and Nebraska it is arguably not), and voter initiatives must be permitted in the state constitution (in Wisconsin they are not). Also, any state adopting an anti-affirmative-action proposal must deal with scores of potential lawsuits protesting the initiatives and testing the parameters of the laws. Therefore, predicting the success and reach of individual state initiatives against racial and gender preferences is difficult. For now, in the private sector and in states without an adverse statute, affirmative action presses on as both a remedy for historical discrimination and a plan for a multicultural future.

CHAPTER 1

Gender

Case Overview

Reed v. Reed (1971)

In a landmark case for the rights of women, a unanimous Supreme Court ruled that preference of one gender over the other is unconstitutional. Chief Justice Warren Burger rendered the decision in the case whereby a minor, Richard Reed, died without a will. His adoptive mother, Sally Reed, who had separated from the adoptive father before the boy's death, filed suit with the probate court to be granted administration of his estate. The father, Cecil Reed, filed a competing petition under pertinent Idaho probate code sections. The probate court ruled that the statutes gave the father a compelling interest, even though the court found both parties equally entitled to act as administrator. Sally Reed appealed to the district court under the Equal Protection Clause of the Fourteenth Amendment. Meanwhile, Cecil Reed appealed to the Idaho Supreme Court, which upheld the probate code specifying male preference in estate administration.

The Supreme Court's decision noted that the probate code gave the right to administer an estate to the father without any consideration of the relative abilities of the competing applicants. And while the Equal Protection Clause of the Fourteenth Amendment allows states the power to treat different classes of people in different ways, such a classification must have a substantial and reasonable relation to the object of the statute. If no justification for a preference exists, then persons in similar circumstances must be treated as equals. Also, no such classification between the sexes can exist if the goal is merely the reduction of workload for a court, as the probate court statute suggests.

Reed v. Reed set the stage for Supreme Court and lower court decisions in subsequent decades not only for affirmative action, but also for other gender discrimination cases involving maternity-leave rules, sexual harassment, and promotion fairness. For the first time in U.S. history, the highest court in the land prohibited discrimination against women. In doing so, the Court set forth legal principles, in the midst of the feminist movement, which guided the force of new ideas regarding the role of women at home and at work. As the Court influenced concepts of equal protection and gender discrimination, the rulings also reflected changing public opinion on the status of women. Within the decade following the *Reed* decision, affirmative action became an effective method for workplace integration of the sexes.

> "To give a mandatory preference to members of either sex over members of the other . . . [is] forbidden by the Equal Protection Clause of the Fourteenth Amendment."

The Court's Decision: Dissimilar Treatment of Men and Women Is Unconstitutional

Warren E. Burger

Warren E. Burger was nominated to the Supreme Court in 1969 by Richard Nixon and served until his retirement in 1986. His tenure on the Court was the longest for a chief justice in the twentieth century.

Chief Justice Warren E. Burger, in this unanimous decision, asserts that a statute ordering mandatory preference to males violates the Equal Protection Clause of the Fourteenth Amendment. The Idaho probate code in question dictated that the right to administer an estate be given to the father without any determination of the relative capabilities of the involved applicants. The chief justice maintains that the Equal Protection Clause does not deny states the power to treat different classes of people in different ways. However, such a classification must have substantial and reasonable criteria related to the object of the statute; otherwise, persons in similar circumstances must be treated equally.

Warren E. Burger, majority opinion, *Reed v. Reed*, 404 U.S. 71, 1971.

Richard Lynn Reed, a minor, died intestate in Ada County, Idaho, on March 29, 1967. His adoptive parents, who had separated sometime prior to his death, are the parties to this appeal. Approximately seven months after Richard's death, his mother, appellant Sally Reed, filed a petition in the Probate Court of Ada County, seeking appointment as administratrix of her son's estate. Prior to the date set for a hearing on the mother's petition, appellee Cecil Reed, the father of the decedent, filed a competing petition seeking to have himself appointed administrator of the son's estate. The probate court held a joint hearing on the two petitions and thereafter ordered that letters of administration be issued to appellee Cecil Reed upon his taking the oath and filing the bond required by law. The court treated 15-312 and 15-314 of the Idaho Code as the controlling statutes and read those sections as compelling a preference for Cecil Reed because he was a male.

Men Given Preference by Statute

Section 15-312 designates the persons who are entitled to administer the estate of one who dies intestate [without a will]. In making these designations, that section lists 11 classes of persons who are so entitled and provides, in substance, that the order in which those classes are listed in the section shall be determinative of the relative rights of competing applicants for letters of administration. One of the 11 classes so enumerated is "[t]he father or mother" of the person dying intestate. Under this section, then, appellant and appellee, being members of the same entitlement class, would seem to have been equally entitled to administer their son's estate. Section 15-314 provides, however, that

> "[o]f several persons claiming and equally entitled [under 15-312] to administer, males must be preferred to females, and relatives of the whole to those of the half blood."

In issuing its order, the probate court implicitly recognized the equality of entitlement of the two applicants under 15-312 and noted that neither of the applicants was under any legal disability; the court ruled, however, that appellee, being a male, was to be preferred to the female appellant "by reason of Section 15-314 of the Idaho Code." In stating this conclusion, the probate judge gave no indication that he had attempted to determine the relative capabilities of the competing applicants to perform the functions incident to the administration of an estate. It seems clear the probate judge considered himself bound by statute to give preference to the male candidate over the female, each being otherwise "equally entitled."

Sally Reed appealed from the probate court order, and her appeal was treated by the District Court of the Fourth Judicial District of Idaho as a constitutional attack on 15-314. In dealing with the attack, that court held that the challenged section violated the Equal Protection Clause of the Fourteenth Amendment and was, therefore, void; the matter was ordered "returned to the Probate Court for its determination of which of the two parties" was better qualified to administer the estate.

Lower Court Rejects Equal Protection Clause Argument

This order was never carried out, however, for Cecil Reed took a further appeal to the Idaho Supreme Court, which reversed the District Court and reinstated the original order naming the father administrator of the estate. In reaching this result, the Idaho Supreme Court first dealt with the governing statutory law and held that under 15-312 "a father and mother are 'equally entitled' to letters of administration," but the preference given to males by 15-314 is "mandatory" and leaves no room for the exercise of a probate court's discretion in the appointment of administrators. Having thus definitively and authoritatively interpreted the statutory provisions involved, the Idaho Supreme Court then proceeded to examine, and reject,

Sally Reed's contention that 15-314 violates the Equal Protection Clause by giving a mandatory preference to males over females, without regard to their individual qualifications as potential estate administrators.

Sally Reed thereupon appealed for review by this Court, and we noted probable jurisdiction: Having examined the record and considered the briefs and oral arguments of the parties, we have concluded that the arbitrary preference established in favor of males by 15-314 of the Idaho Code cannot stand in the face of the Fourteenth Amendment's command that no State deny the equal protection of the laws to any person within its jurisdiction.

Idaho does not, of course, deny letters of administration to women altogether. Indeed, under 15-312, a woman whose spouse dies intestate has a preference over a son, father, brother, or any other male relative of the decedent. Moreover, we can judicially notice that in this country, presumably due to the greater longevity of women, a large proportion of estates, both intestate and under wills of decedents, are administered by surviving widows.

The Equal Protection Clause Applies

Section 15-314 is restricted in its operation to those situations where competing applications for letters of administration have been filed by both male and female members of the same entitlement class established by 15-312. In such situations, 15-314 provides that different treatment be accorded to the applicants on the basis of their sex; it thus establishes a classification subject to scrutiny under the Equal Protection Clause.

In applying that clause, this Court has consistently recognized that the Fourteenth Amendment does not deny to States the power to treat different classes of persons in different ways. The Equal Protection Clause of that amendment does, however, deny to States the power to legislate that different treatment be accorded to persons placed by a statute into different classes on the basis of criteria wholly unrelated to the objective of that statute. A classification "must be reasonable, not arbitrary, and must rest upon some ground of difference having a fair and substantial relation to the object of the legislation, so that all persons similarly circumstanced shall be treated alike." The question presented by this case, then, is whether a difference in the sex of competing applicants for letters of administration bears a rational relationship to a state objective that is sought to be advanced by the operation of 15-312 and 15-314.

Equal Treatment Overrules Probate Court Convenience

In upholding the latter section, the Idaho Supreme Court concluded that its objective was to eliminate one area of controversy when two or more persons, equally entitled under 15-312, seek letters of administration and thereby present the probate court "with the issue of which one should be named." The court also concluded that where such persons are not of the same sex, the elimination of females from consideration "is neither an illogical nor arbitrary method devised by the legislature to resolve an issue that would otherwise require a hearing as to the relative merits ... of the two or more petitioning relatives. . . ."

Clearly the objective of reducing the workload on probate courts by eliminating one class of contests is not without some legitimacy. The crucial question, however, is whether 15-314 advances that objective in a manner consistent with the command of the Equal Protection Clause. We hold that it does not. To give a mandatory preference to members of either sex over members of the other, merely to accomplish the elimination of hearings on the merits, is to make the very kind of arbitrary legislative choice forbidden by the Equal Protection Clause of the Fourteenth Amendment; and whatever may be said as to the positive values of avoiding intrafamily controversy, the choice in this context may not lawfully be mandated solely on the basis of sex.

Dissimilar Treatment by Gender Unconstitutional

We note finally that if 15-314 is viewed merely as a modifying appendage to 15-312 and as aimed at the same objective, its constitutionality is not thereby saved. The objective of 15-312 clearly is to establish degrees of entitlement of various classes of persons in accordance with their varying degrees and kinds of relationship to the intestate. Regardless of their sex, persons within any one of the enumerated classes of that section are similarly situated with respect to that objective. By providing dissimilar treatment for men and women who are thus similarly situated, the challenged section violates the Equal Protection Clause.

> *"Affirmative action has improved lives for many women of color, but it is just beginning to do so."*

Women of Color Face Two Barriers

Laura M. Padilla

Laura M. Padilla is a law professor at California Western School of Law.

In the following selection, Padilla acknowledges that for minority women, affirmative action has proven effective in increasing employment opportunities and access to college. However, she argues that much still needs to be accomplished, especially for women of color in the legal profession, in higher education, and in positions of power generally. According to Padilla, if the benefits offered by affirmative action disappear, then the struggle will become even more difficult.

A common myth is that women of color receive a "double affirmative action benefit" because of their "double outsider" status. A widespread perception is that women of color receive enhanced consideration because of the underrepresentation of both women and people of color in higher education, government contracts, and positions of power generally. For example, "[p]opular belief is that affirmative action is alive and well and that multicultural women attorneys have a double advantage: race and gender." The reality is that while

Laura M. Padilla, "Intersectionality and Positionality: Situating Women of Color in the Affirmative Action Dialogue," *Fordham Law Review*, vol. LXVI, no. 3, December 1997, pp. 843–920. Reproduced by permission.

affirmative action has benefited women of color, sometimes helping them with college admissions and other times allowing them to enter and advance in professions previously closed to them, the barriers for women of color remain strong even with affirmative action. "The combination of being an attorney of color and a woman is a double negative in the legal marketplace, regardless of the type of practice or geographic region involved."

Claims that Affirmative Action Does Not Help Are Wrong

In spite of remaining barriers, there is a fight to terminate affirmative action because of the misconception that it is not working. Some critics argue that affirmative action does not help minorities or women (they are usually silent on women of color), and thus should be terminated. The statistics say otherwise. "As a general matter, increases in the numbers of employees, or students or entrepreneurs from historically underrepresented groups are a measure of increased opportunity." This increased opportunity is not coincidental—over 6 million women have obtained employment opportunities because of affirmative action. Affirmative action's effectiveness becomes clearer when comparing women's membership in various professions before and after its implementation. In the medical profession, women made up 7.6% of all physicians in the United States in 1970, but had increased to 16.9% in 1990. In the legal profession, women made up approximately 3% of all lawyers in the late 1960s, but had increased to 23% in 1994. Furthermore, over the course of a single decade, the number of female attorneys of color went from approximately 7,300 to 23,000. These increases are encouraging, and they demonstrate that affirmative action has been effective for women of color and should continue in effect.

Racial Bias in the Professions

These successes, however, must be tempered with sobering statistics which show that women generally, and women of color especially, have a long way to go. The double-dip myth becomes ever more mythical when considering current statistics. An analysis of women in major New York law firms indicates that while the number of women partners increased steadily throughout the 1980's, "there was a sharp drop-off in new women partners after 1990." In 1995, while 13.43% of the partners in this country's major law firms were women, only 2.79% were minorities. There were no statistics on what percentage of those minority partners were women, but I can safely state that it was fewer than 2.79%. In fact, there are so few partners who are women of color, they are statistically insignificant. In a hearing regarding the glass ceiling, one woman testified that she "found no statistical data concerning promotion of minority women to partnership. They are indeed the invisible minority." One newspaper article explained: "Minority women fare the worst. They have the lowest percentage of entry level jobs in law firms, following white men, white women and minority men." In fact, fewer than 3% of all lawyers and judges are minority women. Note also the dearth of statistics on women of color. They are hard to find because until recently, women of color's existence, much less their particular issues and concerns, had not been discretely considered, and certainly was not doubly celebrated.

Not only are there few attorneys who are women of color, but those who have entered the profession face greater obstacles than either men of color or white women. An ABA committee summarized the reasons as follows: "(1) stereotypes that limit job opportunities, (2) failure to be recognized as competent, (3) failure to advance as rapidly as others, (4) undue difficulties in attaining partnership status, (5) pay inequities, (6) insufficient mentoring, and, (7) heightened scrutiny of hours, work product and performance." The ABA also established a joint project, called the Multicultural Women Attorneys Network ("MWAN"), to study issues of concern to female attorneys of color. It conducted hearings across the country and made the following findings:

The combination of being an attorney of color and a woman is a double negative in the legal marketplace, regardless of the type of practice or geographic region involved; Multicultural women attorneys perceive they are "ghettoized" into certain practice areas and other options are closed or implicitly unavailable; Multicultural women attorneys must repeatedly establish their competence to professors, peers and judges; As evidenced by continuing attitudes and negative stereotypes, multicultural women attorneys are invisible to the profession and have more difficulty achieving prominence and rewards within the legal field; To succeed, multicultural women attorneys must choose between race and gender; and, Minority women lawyers face barriers of gender discrimination in minority bar associations and race discrimination in majority bar associations.

Affirmative action has done a credible job of getting women of color into some power or prestige professions, such as law. It would seem to follow logically that as women entered these fields, they would change their structure and dynamics, making them more hospitable for women generally and women of color specifically. This is not happening, however. While a significant number of women have entered the legal profession over the last twenty years, they have not made as much progress in promotion. Nor are they represented in positions of power in the legal profession. The situation for women of color is obviously worse. Not only do they have to contend with gender bias, they deal with racial bias from majority men and women. Thus, instead of seeing a double advantage, one frequently sees a double negative. "Often, white women attorneys are uncomfortable or unconcerned about addressing race or ethnicity issues. Generally, multicultural women feel ostracized by white women and believe they carry the responsibility of rectifying their own outsider status."

Thus, discrimination as well as other barriers continue to haunt the small percentage of women of color who actually enter the legal profession. Until these barriers are eliminated, affirmative measures are still necessary to enable women of color a chance to succeed in the law.

Black Women Law Students and Lawyers

The situation is not much different for female law students of color. They also suffer from relative invisibility, especially compared to white students who are considered the "norm." In describing the atmosphere at Yale Law School, former students noted that:

Entirely absent were images of women and men of color. These surroundings kept us distrustful, reminding us that the institution that admitted us had traditionally denied entrance to women and people of color. The pictures, the furniture, the male professors—all indicated that the place had always belonged to white men.

One report described the grim experiences of women law students of color "primarily in terms of their battle against the credibility problem, which encompasses both the phenomenon of invisibility and the presumption of incompetence." The process of fading women of color into invisibility occurs on many levels. For example, while they may consider themselves as healthy, whole persons comprised of multiple identifies, female students of color are often asked to excise portions of their identity by being forced to choose between outsider status on the basis of either gender or race. Thus, their wholeness vanishes. Their classmates, law professors, and law school administrators also contribute to this fading and fracturing process. Classmates may exclude them from study groups, clubs, moot court, and advocacy, negotiation, or other competitions, as well as social activities. Law professors are notorious for disproportionately calling upon white males. This is even worse for the female of color who gets the nerve to raise her hand, only to be ignored repeatedly. Even if she is called on, her comments are often overlooked or attributed to someone else. Administrators also contribute to the invisibility of women of color, even if unintentionally. For example, they do not include as many of these students as school spokespersons, as tutors, as advisors, or in other representative capacities. Once again, intersectionality that could be celebrated is instead used against women of color.

The dual burden on women law students of color both perpetuates some patterns that commenced earlier, such as the breeding of self-doubt, and results in new and different forms of silencing. These are the experiences of women law students of color with affirmative action. This speaks of the need to strengthen affirmative action for women of color and to institutionalize multiculturalism so that the entry benefits of affirmative action are not lost in outdated but deeply ingrained institutional racism. Without affirmative action, future generations of attorneys will lack the richness and diversity that women of color bring to the practice, academy, and judiciary, and women of color, the legal system at large, and society as impacted by law will suffer.

Black Women in Higher Education

Women of color are also noticeably absent in leadership roles in higher education. A study on the status of California's higher education pointed out that of its thirty-seven top executives, 70% are white, 14% are African-American, 8% are Latino, and 3% are Asian. While 22% of the executives were women, each chief executive officer was a white male, prompting an analyst to point out that "this group is less diverse than it was a decade ago." The University of California's team of top executives, the most prestigious of California's higher education leadership, was the least diverse, with "no Asians, Latinos, or women [who] serve at the vice president level or above."

In other professions, the doors have barely opened for women, much less women of color. For example, only 3% of firefighters, 8% of police officers, and just over 2% of construction and trades workers are women. The doors to these professions have opened only a crack with affirmative action. Imagine how tightly shut they will be if affirmative action becomes illegal.

Women of Color Benefit from Affirmative Action

It is clear from the information in this section that women of color are not doubly benefiting from affirmative action. While affirmative action has resulted in increased opportunities for women of color, they are still underrepresented in higher education, government contracting, and positions of power across the board. On the same day that I am writing this, I read that women currently hold only "500 of the 7,213 directors' seats of the Fortune 500, or 6.9%, and minorities hold 244 directors' seats, or 3.4%." While this is concededly better than the 0% figure which I would have read about not so long ago, it remains a challenge to get into those positions, and once there, the work has just begun. Many women of color are struggling even with the benefits that affirmative action offers. If affirmative action disappears, opportunities for women of color will decline. Furthermore, women of color who have advanced partly because of affirmative action will need to tread cautiously because protective measures designed to prevent discriminatory behavior may well disappear.

In sum, the information in this section not only exposes the double-benefits myth for what it is—a myth—but more importantly, it magnifies the need for affirmative action for women of color. Affirmative action has improved lives for many women of color, but it is just beginning to do so. It is pivotal at this stage to continue affirmative action programs in order both to allow the women who have entered schools and professions the chance to progress in environments that are not hostile and discriminatory, and to make equal entry opportunities available to more women of color.

> "Poverty remains skewed by gender,
> women still face barriers to full equal-
> ity, and women of all classes struggle
> with integrating work and home."

The Progress of Women
in the Workplace

Vicki Lens

Vicki Lens, J.D., Ph.D is an assistant professor at Columbia University School of Social Work.

The Supreme Court, in its landmark decision in 1971, prohibited discrimination against women. In the following selection, Lens chronicles how the workforce was transformed by working women in the 1970s after the Reed v. Reed *ruling and a series of equal opportunity laws enacted by Congress. She highlights the recognition of sexual harassment as a form of discrimination in the 1980s and the glass ceiling that bars women from gaining positions of power in corporate America.*

In 1971 the Supreme Court held for the first time that the Constitution forbid[s] discrimination against women [*Reed v. Reed*]. Reversing course from the earlier part of the century when it upheld protective legislation limiting women's ability to work, the Court thus entered the national conversation on women's roles sparked by the modern feminist movement. One of its contributions to the debate was to articulate a new set of legal rules to govern expanding notions of equality and gender discrimination in the private sphere of the family and the public sphere of work. . . .

Early Legal Decisions

The Court's view in *Bradwell v. Illinois* that "the natural and proper timidity and delicacy [that] belongs to the female sex evidentially makes her unfit for the occupation of civil life" provides a glimpse into the social constructions of gender during the latter part of the nineteenth century. Modern Supreme Court decisions still draw from such social constructs. A full understanding of these decisions is thus lacking without examining these cultural narratives. Often those narratives are so woven into our consciousness that we fail to see them, just as the justices in *Bradwell* most assuredly contended that they were merely "doing law" when they barred women from the practice of it. . . .

Through these thirty odd years, as more women entered the workplace and male dominated professions, the Court issued forty-one decisions that expanded and contracted women's opportunities and status in the workplace. Using as its source the Constitution and various civil rights laws, including the Equal Pay Act and Title VII of the Civil Rights Act, the Court not only defined equality in the legal sense, but in the cultural, political and social sense as well. As it devised the constitutional test for gender discrimination and interpreted these laws, the Court drew on various non-legal formulations of equality to decide such issues as the equalization of benefits and pay scales, sexual harassment in the workplace and how to treat differences between the sexes. . . .

Change in 1970s

By the 1970s, the women's movement was emerging as a potent force for change. While the 1960s signified the movement's birth, the 1970s was its heyday. Women's rights were a part of the national political landscape, with laws, a federal agency and women's organizations, such as NOW, a presence in Washington. Both Democrats and Republicans professed support for women's rights. Public opinion had also begun to shift. By the early 1970s, "women's liberation had become a household word" and nearly 40% of women were in favor of "most efforts to strengthen and change women's status in society."

In sharp contrast to the Civil Rights Act, where gender was an afterthought, the 1970s brought a rash of legislation aimed at helping women achieve equality in such diverse areas as sports, science, employment and financial services, to name a few. Examples include Title IX of the Civil Rights Act that prohibited sex discrimination in any educational program that received federal funds, 1972 amendments to the Equal Pay Act that extended coverage to more occupations, the Equal Credit Opportunity Act, which prohibited discrimination in credit transactions, and the Women's Education Equity Act of 1974 that provided grants and programs to eliminate stereotypes and achieve educational equity. In 1972 Congress also passed the Equal Rights Amendment, the centerpiece of the women's rights movement during this decade.

The workplace was also transformed during the 1970s. The number of working women increased from 43.3% in 1970 to 51.2% in 1980; thus for the first time "there were more women in the labor force than out of it." Most women worked in gender segregated occupations such as teaching, nursing and clerical work, but were excluded from such male dominated professions such as law, medicine and blue-collar work, including the construction trade, fire departments and prison systems. Women viewed employment in these occupations as providing a living wage, in contrast to the low wages found in the "pink ghetto." Also, unlike clerical work, which served the needs of a typically male employer, and hence replicated women's roles at home, these jobs offered autonomy and self-sufficiency. With unions sometimes hesitant to support women, informal and independent work caucuses emerged to challenge gender-segregated occupations and leading to the formation of more organized advocacy groups such as 9-5. During this decade, affirmative action was also viewed as the primary and most effective mechanism for redrawing and integrating the workplace. According to feminist historian Nancy MacLean, "occupational segregation . . . declined more in the decade from 1970 to 1980, the peak years of affirmative action enforcement, than in any other comparable period in U.S. history." . . .

Change in the 1980s

The 1980s began with the election of a Republican president, Ronald Reagan, who unlike past presidents was hostile to women's rights, choosing to cater to his party's increasingly conservative faction. Feminist historians Ferree and Hess describe "the major challenges of the 1980s [as] including maintaining public approval for positions that a popular president and the federal government no longer supported." This included a Justice Department that pulled back on the enforcement of equal opportunity statutes and Supreme Court decisions that made discrimination harder to prove. Affirmative action also came under attack with Presidents Reagan and [George H.W] Bush actively campaigning against it.

Economically, women, particularly poor women and African American women, did not fare well during this decade. Inequality grew as wages remained depressed and tax cuts to the wealthy failed to "trickle down" to the bottom of the economic ladder where nearly half of the female labor force was concentrated. With poor women getting poorer and welfare programs getting stingier, the feminization of poverty continued to increase. Squeezed by a labor market that exploited low wageworkers and cutbacks in social services programs women found it increasingly difficult to earn a living wage or care for their families.

Women at the higher end of the economic ladder also faced obstacles. Their advancement in male-dominated occupations was stymied. A new phrase entered the lexicon "the glass ceiling" to denote the invisible barrier women confronted when climbing the corporate ladder. As surveys during the decade demonstrated, men still overwhelmingly (95%–97%) comprised senior management and executive positions in the nation's largest corporations and although the disparity between women's and men's wages decreased during the decade, by its end women were still earning only seventy-four cents to a man's dollar.

New approaches to increasing women's wages were implemented during the 1980s. Whereas in the 1970s women entered previously male occupations as a way to eliminate the wage gender gap, in the 1980s women used the principle of pay equity to increase the pay and status of traditionally female occupations. The concept of pay equity or comparable worth meant that jobs involving similar skill levels, effort, working conditions, and level of responsibility would be compensated at the same rate of pay. This highlighted the inequity of paying teachers, nurses and secretaries less than, for example, the typical male jobs of tree trimmers or sign painters. While the idea did not take hold across the labor force, by the end of the decade many state governments, and some local ones, had adopted comparable worth policies.

During the 1980s a new form of discrimination, sexual harassment, was recognized in the workplace. First identified by feminist legal scholar Catharine A. Mackinnon, sexual harassment "refers to the unwanted imposition of sexual requirements in the context of a relationship of unequal power." Initially sexual harassment was viewed as a personal problem not relevant to the workplace. The first sexual harassment lawsuits brought in the mid-1970s were unsuccessful, although within a few years these cases were reversed and sexual harassment was defined as a form of sexual discrimination under Title VII. Surveys conducted in the beginning of the 1980s confirmed that sexual harassment was a common occurrence in many workplaces. The first federal survey, conducted in 1980 by the U.S. Merit Systems Protection Board found that 40% of female federal employees surveyed had been victims of sexual harassment. Throughout the decade such diverse groups as university faculty and staff, blue-collar workers, attorneys and the airline industry identified sexual harassment as a problem. Sexual harassment was broadened to include, in addition to requesting sexual favors in exchange for jobs, promotions, and other job related benefits, the creation of a hostile work environment, which made it difficult for women to perform their jobs. Despite the legal and social recognition of sexual harassment, many businesses were hesitant to implement sexual harassment policies or grievance procedures. Nonetheless, behavior that had in an earlier decade been either ignored or accepted as an inevitable product of a gender-integrated workplace was now considered unlawful. . . .

Change in the 1990s

The glass ceiling still dominated discussions about women's employment opportunities as evidenced by the passage of the Glass Ceiling Act (part of the Civil Rights Act of 1991), mandating the establishment of a Glass Ceiling Commission to examine barriers to women and minority advancement in corporate America and formulate a strategic plan to overcome it. The Commission found a litany of barriers demonstrating that, despite women's gains over the past decades, a thick residue of discrimination and bias remained. They included corporate climates that alienated and isolated women, the failure to recruit, mentor or train women for higher positions, biased rating, performance and testing systems and harassment by colleagues. The Commission also noted the "lack of vigorous, consistent monitoring and law enforcement."

At the decade's end, there was considerable evidence that the glass ceiling had still not been shattered; the proportion of women corporate officers in the 500 largest corporations was only 12% in 1999. And while inroads have been made in professions such as medicine and law, women still remain, for the most part segregated by occupation and concentrated in the service industries. The majority of minimum wageworkers are women.

The status of poor women also declined in the 1990s. In 1996, the Aid to Families with Dependent Children program was replaced with the Temporary Assistance to Needy Families (TANF), a time-limited and work-focused program that requires women to work up to thirty-five hours per week. This finalized the new norm of motherhood, introduced in the late 1960s, where women were wageworkers rather than stay at home mothers. For poor women, as in the past, this meant low wage work, and a lack of adequate resources such as day care.

The 1990s also marked the first legislation directly addressing the competing demands of work and parenting. Unlike other industrialized countries, women's struggle for equality in the United States did not encompass the notion that it was society's collective responsibility to help families balance work and home. The Family and Medical Leave Act, passed in 1993, was the first law to address this idea by permitting up to twelve weeks unpaid leave of absence for both women and men for family needs. Although much less generous than benefits granted in other countries, feminists viewed the law as a major victory.

The 1990s were also notable for gains in the political arena. Women increased their representation in state legislatures from 17% in 1989 to 22.6% in 2002. The biggest gains were at the federal level, with the number of women in the Senate increasing from 2 in 1999 to 13 in 2002, and in the House from 23 to 73. In 1992, women surpassed men in electoral participation making up 54% percent of all voters.

After four decades of struggle, the legal, social, political and cultural landscape for women was transformed. Women are now expected to work for at least some portion of their adult life and at more and varied types of jobs. They are also engaged in political life in greater numbers. In many respects feminist ideology has become mainstream as the separate spheres ideology becomes more marginalized. Despite these gains, the basic conundrums that confronted feminists in the early part of the century remain unresolved. The "difference" debate continues: should biological, cultural or socially based differences be leveled, celebrated or ignored? Poverty remains skewed by gender, women still face barriers to full equality, and women of all classes struggle with integrating work and home. . . .

For the last thirty odd years, the Court, along with the rest of us, has puzzled over the connection between equality and gender. At a critical juncture in the feminist movement, this inquiry has interjected itself into many of the most contentious public disputes of the day. Should pregnancy be ignored or accommodated in the workplace? What doors should be opened for women, and which should remain shut? How should the economic pie be divided among men and women? Who should bear the burden of the costs of equality? . . .

Changing Supreme Court Analyses

What were some of the conclusions and observations drawn from this discourse to provide insight into the Court's workings? Most noticeable is the Court's fluidity in choosing from the various formulations of equality and separate spheres ideology through the years and sometimes even within the same case. While the Court oscillated among different versions of equality, using substantive equality to give a little more (military promotions, affirmative action, and Social Security benefits) and formal equality to level sex-based distinctions in public programs (widows and mothers Social Security benefits, Worker's Compensation, and Unemployment Insurance), it also, with some regularity, abandoned the equality framework. This was most apparent in the early years, the 1970s, during a period of rapid change and reorientation of sex roles. The Court's ambivalence and confusion toward these changes was evident when it prevented employers from refusing to hire women with school-age children, but then stated it might be appropriate if family obligations were shown to interfere. Similarly, the pregnancy cases had the Court tied up in knots, as it bounced from denying pregnancy was related to gender, to calling it a burden unique to women.

The Court also occasionally advanced the more radical strands of feminist theory when it used difference theory language to require that men be admitted to an all female nursing school and when leveling men and women's pay scales.

At other times the Court hesitated pushing the cultural lines too far forward, abandoning its equality framework and reverting to a separate spheres frame when women asked to enter the roughest domains of men—all male prisons and the military. While this trend diminished in later decades, as exemplified by the opening of all male military college to women, the sexual harassment cases that preoccupied the Court throughout the last decade-and-a-half showed a Court caught between the frames of non-subordination and separate spheres. Yes, sexual harassment was a work, not personal issue and an abusive use of male power, but the Court still required women to file a complaint against that very power structure in order to be compensated for it.

The Court was also most likely to abandon an equality framework when the interests of an identified group of men were at risk. Beginning with veterans preference programs, it rendered women invisible in the workplace by refusing to recognize the connection between discrimination in the military, veterans preference programs and women's second class status in state government. Later on, collective bargaining agreements trumped EEOC conciliation agreements and seniority rights could be denied to victims of discrimination when it worked against men's interests and job status. The one major exception was in the area of affirmative action, although the Court took pains to argue that no man was specifically harmed.

The Court also hesitated in imposing certain remedies after it found a violation of equality, calibrating how far it thought society should go monetarily in compensating for discrimination. This was most notable in the pension cases when, while recognizing the harm, the Court explicitly citing the high cost of doing so, declined to order full redress. Cost also played a substantial role in the pregnancy disability cases, with the Court using it as a reason for not including pregnancy in disability plans.

As the Court applied the various frames of equality or separate spheres ideology, its narratives shifted. When arguing for formal, substantive equality or difference theory, the Court used often impassioned language admonishing against stereotyping, encouraging women to be treated as individuals and bemoaning and even ridiculing past social mores about women. Throughout the 1970s and into the 1980s it redefined the workplace to include working women as a norm entitled to be treated as equal to men and to be compensated for past discrimination.

Then, beginning in the mid-1980s, the Court delved into reshaping workplace behavioral norms by labeling sexual harassment as a work issue and criticizing the double standard that required women to act like "ladies" as they traversed the corporate ladder.

| "[T]he emphasis of affirmative action historically has been on blacks more so than white women."

White Women Do Not Gain an Advantage Through Affirmative Action

James Button, Ryan Bakker, and Barbara A. Rienzo

James Button and Barbara A. Rienzo are professors in the Department of Political Science at the University of Florida. Ryan Bakker is a political science professor at the University of North Carolina at Chapel Hill.

In the following selection, Button, Rienzo, and Bakker reveal the results of an employment study in six southern cities, demonstrating that affirmative action had no impact on the employment of white women. They explain that, traditionally, affirmative action has emphasized blacks over women, which has thus helped blacks in job competition with women. In the studied communities, however, white women held a higher percentage of jobs than any other race or gender, particularly in the service-oriented economy. They conclude that white women are achieving employment at such a level that they do not need to rely on affirmative action.

In the attempt to help women deal with employment barriers and create greater equity in the job market, the federal government enacted legislation to prohibit sex discrimination

James Button, Ryan Bakker, and Barbara A. Rienzo, "White Women and Affirmative Action in Employment in Six Southern Cities," *Social Science Journal*, vol. 43, 2006, pp. 297–302. Copyright © 2006 Published by Elsevier Inc. Reproduced with permission from Elsevier.

and provide greater job opportunities for women. Affirmative action was one of these government programs, and while its focus has primarily been on African Americans, white women are also included in this controversial policy. However, there have been few empirical studies exploring the extent to which affirmative action affects white females either in getting jobs or gaining promotion. The purpose of this study is to investigate this possible policy impact, and to do so in the South where traditional gender-role norms are still prevalent and blacks are perceived as the most disadvantaged group in the job market.

Since the 1970s, affirmative action has required employers to seek out and give preference to women and minorities in occupations where they are under-represented. The effects of affirmative action on white women's success in the job market are difficult to assess because the period of implementation of affirmative action in the 1970s and 1980s coincided with the rapid increase of women in the labor force. Throughout the 1980s and 1990s, white women's progress in the labor market and increased earnings seemed to be due to better education and more work experience, factors unrelated to affirmative action.

Popular Assumption

The popular assumption is that white women have been the primary beneficiaries of affirmative action. The basis for this argument is the assertion that because white women are the best educated among disadvantaged groups, employers have been more likely to hire them under affirmative action guidelines. Evidence for this is the substantial gains women have made in the job market since the late 1970s, including in high-level management positions and in the professions of law and medicine. Furthermore, a major survey of employers in four major cities indicated that firms with affirmative action policies were 15% more likely to have hired white women, even controlling for other factors that affected hiring decisions.

Other social scientists take a less sanguine view of the role of affirmative action. Affirmative action has become such a controversial and politically divisive policy that it is no longer able to secure the public support necessary to be effective. These political forces have resulted in a lack of enforcement and a backlog of cases for federal enforcement agencies that have severely limited the influence of affirmative action policy. Moreover G.C. Loury contends that there is much less sex discrimination today, due mainly to the 1964 Civil Rights Act and other legislation, so that women can achieve employment without government assistance.

Explanatory Variables

It is important to look at affirmative action in the context of other employment-related factors. Larger businesses (size), as measured by number of employees, are more likely to hire disadvantaged groups than small businesses. Large firms pay higher wages and benefits and, therefore, attract more applicants. National and regional-affiliated businesses attract and employ more minorities than do locally owned firms (type). National or regional firms express a greater visibility and concern for the importance of diversity, as well as a larger fear of lawsuits and negative press coverage if women are refused employment. Additionally, the kind of business may impact the employment of white women. Industries, retail stores, and restaurants are relatively open to the public and more committed to a diverse work force than traditionally segregated businesses like financial institutions (banks, real estate, insurance) and private recreational businesses (bowling alleys and country clubs). The location of businesses, in terms of proximity to black and other minority neighborhoods, may expose white women to added competition for jobs. Businesses with many white female customers are also more likely to hire and promote white women in order to improve social interactions and thereby boost female business.

More formal methods of recruitment, including newspaper ads and employment services, may favor white women and other minorities because they reduce potential employer prejudices. White women and minority employers often evaluate white female applicants favorably in terms of social, or interpersonal, skills and therefore see them as especially qualified for employment in a service-oriented job market. Moreover, these "soft" skills are employee traits that are often preferred over formal credentials or "hard" skills. To measure affirmative action policies, we asked employers "Do you personally support affirmative action as a policy to give preferences to blacks and females in hiring and promotion?" and scored their responses on a 3-point scale (0 = no; 1 = yes, somewhat; 2 = yes, a lot).

Finally, the supply side of the labor market is important as well. Larger proportions of white females as job applicants, as well as greater numbers of females in managerial positions, provide a boost to the employment of women. However, employer perceptions that some women are not well qualified, perhaps due to increases in applicants who are recent welfare recipients with little education, may hinder females. Another demographic factor [a]ffecting white female jobholding in the South is the possible competition with African Americans vying for employment.

This study is composed of six Florida cities. The cities are relatively small (average population size of 27,732 with a range from 7,000 to 64,000) and thus typical in size to most southern cities. . . .

Results

White women compete well in the job markets of these communities. Indeed, white women hold a higher percentage of jobs overall (37%) than any other race/gender group, although white males (33%) and African Americans (26%) are not far behind. Hispanics are a small proportion of the population in these cities (4%) and therefore hold relatively few jobs. The figure for white women in our sample of businesses is only slightly higher than the 2000 U.S. Census reports for these cities which show 31% of the labor force (age 16 and over) is composed of white women.

White men dominate higher-level professional and managerial positions (49%), with white women holding 35% of these jobs. Blacks are a distant third, with only 14% employed at this high level despite blacks making up 38% of the labor force. At the skilled/semi-skilled level of employment, white women constitute 36%, slightly higher than white men (32%) and blacks (28%). At the lower job echelons of unskilled/menial laborers, such as motel housekeepers, restaurant dishwashers, and other manual laborers, white women number 25%. Blacks dominate this job category (41%), as they have historically in the South. . . .

The results indicate that the percentage of job applicants who are white women is the variable most highly and directly related to the level of female employment at all job levels. The results show that the greater the application efforts by white women to secure jobs, the more likely they are to be hired since they are perceived by most employers as good workers. Another factor that is consistently and strongly related to white female employment is the kind of business. This variable shows a positive relationship for employment at all levels except for professional/managerial jobs. This indicates that retail stores, restaurants and industries are most likely to employ white women, and this is the case for most employment levels. The most surprising finding is the high, negative relationships between black and white female employment. In every model this finding is apparent. Clearly there is intense job competition between these two disadvantaged groups. Moreover, 21%

of employers claimed that there was a lack of qualified white females to hire, a finding that significantly reduced female employment.

Our main interest here is the role of affirmative action. The results indicate that affirmative action was not significantly related to any level of white female employment when controlling for other variables.... Clearly affirmative action has no impact on women's employment status.

Limitations and Successes

White women do very well in the private job market of these southern cities. Indeed, they outnumber white men and African Americans in the new service-oriented economy. Only at the higher levels of employment do white men continue to dominate the labor market. In terms of explanatory factors, white female job applicants, and the kinds of businesses are resource and contextual variables that are highly related to white female employment. A barrier to such employment, however, is the view by some employers that there is a lack of qualified white female applicants.

A more serious limitation for white women's employability is competition with African Americans. In the South, this finding is not surprising since blacks make up a relatively large proportion of the population and labor force. While blacks are disproportionately found at lower skill levels than white women, blacks compete with women at the professional/managerial level as well. Affirmative action is one factor that has assisted African Americans in job competition with women. A previous study supports this finding in that employer support for affirmative action had a positive, significant relationship with black employment, particularly at higher job levels.

So why haven't white women been helped by affirmative action? The success of white female workers suggests they need no help. White women, compared with most blacks and

Latinos, have greater education credentials and higher levels of required job skills, both of which make them more qualified in today's job market. Moreover, the emphasis of affirmative action historically has been on blacks more so than white women. The Equal Employment Opportunity Commission (EEOC), the primary federal enforcement agency for affirmative action, has not perceived that sex discrimination is its primary mission, especially in the South. Furthermore, affirmative action as a policy was conceived during the 1960s civil rights movement and was originally intended to create greater opportunities for blacks. Even following the Reagan Administration's weakened enforcement of affirmative action, there was still greater attention by EEOC to race rather than sex discrimination in employment. Finally, employers associate affirmative action primarily with blacks. Our interviews with business owners and managers indicated this, and other studies have shown this to be true as well. Thus while affirmative action may not be affecting white female laborers, white women have nonetheless proved successful in gaining jobs and influencing changes in the workplace that benefit all women.

"*[I]ndividuals cannot be excluded from educational institutions based solely on their gender.*"

Affirmative Action for Men

Debra Franzese

Debra Franzese is a law student at American University, Washington College of Law, and a junior staff member of the American University Law Review.

In the following selection, Franzese observes that although the Supreme Court has ruled on the constitutionality of race-based affirmative action programs, the Court has not yet addressed the question of gender-based affirmative action programs. Since the Equal Protection Clause of the Fourteenth Amendment covers only state action, women cannot sue private colleges that favor male students. While the Court considers race a "suspect" classification warranting strict scrutiny under the Equal Protection Clause, the Court has not held that gender is a "suspect" classification. Therefore, intermediate scrutiny, a less stringent judicial review, is applied. In addition to the Equal Protection Clause, Title IX of the Education Amendments of 1972 prohibits sex discrimination in all colleges and universities that receive federal funding. The author points out that some federal courts have ruled that strict scrutiny applies under Title IX when examining discriminatory policies in higher education.

Debra Franzese, "The Gender Curve: An Analysis of Colleges' Use of Affirmative Action Policies to Benefit Male Applicants," *American University Law Review*, vol. 56, no. 3, February 2007, pp. 719–50. Copyright © 2007 American University Law Review. Reproduced by permission.

Females currently constitute approximately fifty-seven percent of students on college campuses nationwide, and the Department of Education predicts that this gender gap will increase to nearly sixty percent female by 2010. Instead of cause for celebration, this lack of proportionality has become a source of concern for admissions officers and news commentators.

Growing concern over this gender gap has led some colleges to give male students an edge in the admissions process. For example, the University of Georgia ("UGA") implemented an affirmative action policy that awarded additional points to male applicants. However, when challenged, UGA's policy was declared unconstitutional. Additionally, in March 2006, an admissions officer from Kenyon College published an op-ed article in the *New York Times* about the impact the gender gap has on the admissions process. She declared that because of demographic concerns, admissions committees consider males more valuable candidates than females. While many college administrators do not openly admit to implementing male affirmative action policies, evidence suggests that, in certain circumstances, admissions officers give males an edge in the admissions process. In addition, many colleges have begun targeted campaigns to lure more males to campus. . . .

The Equal Protection Clause provides one method of redress for female students to challenge affirmative action policies that benefit male students. While the Supreme Court has addressed the constitutionality of race-based affirmative action programs, the Court has not yet ruled on the issue of gender-based affirmative action policies.

The Equal Protection Clause and Race-Based Affirmative Action Cases

The Equal Protection Clause of the Fourteenth Amendment declares that "no state shall . . . deny to any person within its jurisdiction the equal protection of the laws." The Supreme

Court interprets the Fourteenth Amendment to regulate only state action, which places private discrimination beyond its reach. Therefore, under the Equal Protection Clause females can only challenge public colleges' affirmative action policies that benefit male students.

The Supreme Court applies different standards of review to analyze policies that discriminate against individuals based on certain characteristics. The Court recognizes race as a suspect classification and applies strict scrutiny to evaluate policies that discriminate against individuals based on this immutable characteristic. Strict scrutiny is also used to evaluate programs that benefit racial minorities, including racial affirmative action policies. To be constitutional, a policy that discriminates against individuals on the basis of race must be narrowly tailored to further a compelling government interest.

The Supreme Court has addressed universities' use of racial affirmative action policies on numerous occasions. The Court first addressed this issue in *Regents of the University of California v. Bakke*. In that case, the Court held that it was unconstitutional for the university to reserve a fixed number of seats in the incoming class for racial minorities; however, the Court expressed approval for the use of race as one factor that admissions officers could consider when evaluating applicants. The Court recognized that offering admission to students with different racial backgrounds constitutes only part of achieving diversity and that using racial quotas to achieve diversity could undermine this goal.

More recently, the Court addressed the issue of racial affirmative action programs in *Grutter v. Bollinger* and *Gratz v. Bollinger*. In *Grutter*, the Court considered the constitutionality of the University of Michigan Law School's affirmative action policy to enroll a "critical mass" of racial minorities in order to foster diversity in the incoming class. The Court held that diversity in a law school setting constituted a compelling state interest, and that the affirmative action policy was narrowly tailored because it conducted an individualized evaluation of each student's application.

While the Court upheld the law school's affirmative action policy in *Grutter*, in *Gratz* it found the program used by the undergraduate institution unconstitutional. The Court accepted the goal of diversity as a compelling state interest; however, the program failed the narrowly tailored prong because the policy awarded twenty points to every minority applicant based solely on his or her race. Both *Grutter* and *Gratz* emphasize the need for colleges to conduct individualized evaluations of each applicant. While schools may use race as a factor, race cannot be the decisive factor in the admissions decision.

The Equal Protection Clause and the Court's Gender Jurisprudence

The Equal Protection Clause also prohibits gender discrimination, although the Supreme Court analyzes gender-based policies under intermediate scrutiny. While the Court has not yet addressed the issue of gender-based affirmative action policies that benefit male applicants, the Court's opinions in *United States v. Virginia* (*VMI*) and *Mississippi University for Women v. Hogan* provide a framework to analyze colleges' use of gender in admission decisions. These opinions emphasize the need to conduct a searching judicial inquiry of the school's asserted goal to ensure that the rationale does not rely on stereotypes about the capabilities of males and females.

Intermediate Scrutiny

A gender-based affirmative action policy would likely be evaluated under a lesser standard of scrutiny than race-based affirmative action because a majority of the Court has never identified gender as a suspect classification. As mentioned above, the Court analyzes gender classifications under intermediate scrutiny, which requires that the policy be substantially related to an important government interest. In *VMI*, the Court held that the government must have an "exceedingly persuasive justification" for a policy that distinguishes among individuals based solely on their gender. Some commentators have argued that this standard of review is more demanding than traditional intermediate scrutiny, but this issue remains an open question until the Court next decides another gender discrimination case. Based on the Court's recent gender discrimination jurisprudence, colleges would need to have an exceedingly persuasive justification to implement an affirmative action program that benefited male students and prove that the plan was substantially related to its asserted goal.

In *VMI*, the Court held that Virginia Military Institute's policy that denied admission to female students violated the Equal Protection Clause. VMI asserted that the institution contributed to educational diversity by offering students the option to attend a single-sex university. The Court, however, rejected VMI's justification because at the time of the university's inception, single-sex education for male students was the primary model of higher education in the United States. In addition, the Court held that VMI's assertion that the admission of women would destroy its reliance on its adversative teaching method did not constitute an exceedingly persuasive justification because the school's rationale for retaining the male-only admissions policy was based upon stereotypes about women's abilities.

Court Rules Against
Gender-Based Exclusion

The Court's holding in *VMI* reaffirmed its decision in *Mississippi University for Women v. Hogan* that individuals cannot be excluded from educational institutions based solely on their gender. In *Hogan*, the Court held that the Mississippi University for Women's policy of excluding male students from its nursing school violated the Equal Protection Clause. The

Court rejected the university's asserted goal of affirmative action for women because nursing is an occupation traditionally dominated by females. The university's policy also failed the second prong of the inquiry; it did not substantially relate to the preservation of the school's educational mission because the school failed to provide evidence that male students' presence in the classroom would adversely affect female students' performance.

Affirmative Action Policies under Title IX of the Education Amendments of 1972

In addition to the Equal Protection Clause, Title IX of the Education Amendments of 1972 provides a statutory framework for female students to challenge affirmative action policies that benefit male applicants. Title IX claims are often brought in conjunction with Equal Protection claims and could potentially provide a higher level of scrutiny.

Title IX prohibits sex discrimination in all educational institutions that receive federal funding. Although Title IX contains absolute language about the prohibition on sex discrimination in all educational institutions, there are eight exceptions to this broad coverage. One of these exceptions relates to discriminatory admissions policies and limits the statute's coverage, at the undergraduate level, to public coeducational institutions. Consequently, Title IX, which usually provides greater protection than the Equal Protection Clause, provides a limited remedy in the context of discriminatory admissions policies.

Some Federal Courts Apply Strict Scrutiny

Some federal courts have granted female students greater protection under Title IX by applying strict scrutiny to evaluate schools' discriminatory policies. These courts have interpreted Title IX to provide greater protection than the Equal Protection Clause by analogizing it to Title VI of the Civil Rights

Act, which prohibits the use of race discrimination by any program that receives monetary assistance from the federal government. Since Title IX and Title VI have nearly identical wording except for the designation of the protected class, many courts look to legal opinions analyzing Title VI when interpreting Title IX. These courts have concluded that Title IX's legislative history supports the proposition that Congress assumed the statutory interpretation of Title IX would follow Title VI. For example, in *Jeldness v. Pearce*, the United States Court of Appeals for the Ninth Circuit held that since the statutes contained nearly identical language, the same level of protection should be accorded to both protected classes—race and gender.

Affirmative Action Policy Violates Title IX

Recently, in *Johnson v. Board of Regents of University System of Georgia* (*Johnson I*) the United States District Court for the Southern District of Georgia used strict scrutiny to evaluate a gender discrimination claim challenging the University of Georgia's ("UGA") affirmative action policy. UGA awarded an additional quarter point to all male students' academic indices and a half point to all minority students' academic indices. The court held that this affirmative action policy that favored males violated Title IX. This decision, which predates *Grutter* and *Gratz*, declined to recognize diversity in education as a compelling state interest because the university failed to provide quantitative or qualitative evidence to support its program. The district court did not address whether the plan was narrowly tailored because the court concluded that the goal of diversity was "so inherently formless and malleable that no plan can be narrowly tailored to fit it."

Since UGA's affirmative action plan provided a bonus to minority and male applicants, the district court's opinion addressed both issues. The district court used strict scrutiny to evaluate both the racial and gender preferences. The court found that UGA's admissions director could not articulate any need for gender diversity other than a basic assertion that "the state of Georgia is 49th in the country in the percentage of baccalaureate degrees going to males." The district court further explained that "gender preferencing would not even survive the less rigorous intermediate scrutiny [because] ... the desire to 'help out' men who are not earning baccalaureate degrees in the same numbers as women ... is far from persuasive." Since the parties did not raise the gender issue on appeal, the United States Court of Appeals for the Eleventh Circuit focused on the constitutionality of the race-based preference, whereas the district court's opinion provides a preliminary analysis of the danger of using affirmative action policies to benefit male students. The Eleventh Circuit declined to address the issue of whether diversity constituted a compelling interest and instead evaluated whether the plan was narrowly tailored.

The circuit court implemented a four-factor test to evaluate whether the plan satisfied the narrowly tailored requirement. The opinion emphasized the importance of flexibility in the admissions program and explained that the goal of diversity should not constitute an end in itself, but rather a means for achieving the broad mix of cultures and ideas represented in society. The Eleventh Circuit held that the policy was not narrowly tailored since it provided a rigid set of points to minority applicants without an individual determination of their contribution to the school's goal of diversity.

CHAPTER 2

Housing

Case Overview

Arlington Heights v. Metropolitan Housing Corp. (1977)

Although later Supreme Court decisions would focus on the level of examination of an affirmative-action plan, the majority opinion in *Arlington Heights v. Metropolitan Housing Corp.* stressed the intent of the parties accused of discrimination, in this case, the Village of Arlington Heights board in a suburb of Chicago.

Metropolitan Housing Development Corporation (MHDC), a nonprofit developer, contracted to purchase a tract of land to build racially integrated housing for low- and moderate-income families. The MHDC applied to the town for rezoning of the area from single-family to multiple-family classification. The units were to use federal housing subsidies under the National Housing Act, which required the development to be racially integrated. The board denied the rezoning request. The board cited four reasons for rejecting the development. First, the board concluded that the area must maintain the tradition of the neighboring single-family dwellings. Second, the owners of the homes in the neighboring area purchased or built their homes with the assurance that the area would remain a single-family neighborhood. Third, the rezoning threatened to adversely affect the property value of those neighboring sites. And fourth, village policy stated that multiunit zoning had been designed to serve as a buffer between single-family sites and commercial and manufacturing districts. The proposed rezoning development did not meet this requirement since no such districts abutted the parcel of land intended for rezoning.

When the Village of Arlington Heights denied the request for rezoning, MHDC and potential housing inhabitants sued, alleging racial discrimination and violation of the Equal Protection Clause of the Fourteenth Amendment. While the district court agreed with the village board in its attempt to maintain property value and the integrity of the zoning plan, the court of appeals reversed, concluding that the effect of the denial was racially discriminatory, especially since the area was already highly segregated.

Justice Lewis Powell delivered the opinion of the Court, declaring that proof of a racially discriminatory intent or purpose is required to show a violation of the Equal Protection Clause of the Fourteenth Amendment. Moreover, it is the burden of the respondents, the MHDC and potential residents, to prove that racial unfairness was the intended motivation of the board in denying the rezoning request. Justice Powell added that racially disproportionate impact alone is not unconstitutional. Such impact must be considered, but it alone does not render an act racially discriminatory. Several factors, besides racially disproportionate impact, must be considered. Invidious motivation may be shown by actions that demonstrate racism; such evidence may be found in the historical background of the challenged decision, the specific events leading up to the decision, departures from normal procedures, and contemporary statements of the decision makers.

Despite *Arlington Heights* and its mandate for proving racist intent, the Supreme Court has not overruled earlier court decisions. In 1948, the Supreme Court in *Shelly v. Kraemer* held that racially restrictive covenants in housing deeds are unenforceable. And in 1968, the Supreme Court ruled in *Jones v. Mayer* that federal law bars all racial discrimination, public or private, in the sale or rental of property. Therefore, those rulings still carry force without any finding of intent.

> "Proof of racially discriminatory intent
> or purpose is required to show a viola-
> tion of the Equal Protection Clause."

The Court's Decision: Discriminatory Intent Must Be Proven

Lewis F. Powell Jr.

Lewis F. Powell Jr. served fifteen years on the Supreme Court. The centrist judge was appointed to the Court by President Nixon in 1971.

Justice Lewis Powell, in his majority decision regarding a proposed housing development, held that proof of racially discriminatory intent is necessary to show a violation of the Equal Protection Clause of the Fourteenth Amendment. An action will not be held unconstitutional solely because it results in a racially disproportionate result; instead, such a result is merely one of the factors to be considered. Justice Powell states that it must be proven that intent to achieve racial discrimination was a motivating factor for the action to be deemed a violation of the Equal Protection Clause. To determine if such racist factors exist, a reviewing court may look for a clear pattern of official action that can only be explained by racial discrimination. Also, historical background may determine discriminatory intent, especially if a series of events leading up to the challenge reflect racially offensive goals. Nonetheless, the applicant bears the burden of proving racist intent on the part of the decision maker.

Lewis F. Powell Jr., majority opinion, *Arlington Heights v. Metropolitan Housing Corp.*, 429 U.S. 252, 1977.

In 1971 respondent Metropolitan Housing Development Corporation (MHDC) applied to petitioner, the Village of Arlington Heights, Ill., for the rezoning of a 15-acre parcel from single-family to multiple-family classification. Using federal financial assistance, MHDC planned to build 190 clustered townhouse units for low- and moderate-income tenants. The Village denied the rezoning request. MHDC, joined by other plaintiffs who are also respondents here, brought suit in the United States District Court for the Northern District of Illinois. They alleged that the denial was racially discriminatory and that it violated, inter alia, the Fourteenth Amendment and the Fair Housing Act of 1968. Following a bench trial, the District Court entered judgment for the Village, and respondents appealed. The Court of Appeals for the Seventh Circuit reversed, finding that the "ultimate effect" of the denial was racially discriminatory, and that the refusal to rezone therefore violated the Fourteenth Amendment. We granted the Village's petition for certiorari, and now reverse. . . .

New Development Would Bring Affordable Housing

Respondent Ransom, a Negro, works at the Honeywell factory in Arlington Heights and lives approximately 20 miles away in Evanston in a 5-room house with his mother and his son. The complaint alleged that he seeks and would qualify for the housing MHDC wants to build in Arlington Heights. Ransom testified at trial that if Lincoln Green were built he would probably move there, since it is closer to his job.

The injury Ransom asserts is that his quest for housing nearer his employment has been thwarted by official action that is racially discriminatory. If a court grants the relief he seeks, there is at least a "substantial probability," *Warth v. Seldin*, supra, at 504, that the Lincoln Green project will materialize, affording Ransom the housing opportunity he desires in Arlington Heights. . . .

Racially Disproportionate Impact Considered but Not Controlling

Our decision last Term in *Washington v. Davis*, made it clear that official action will not be held unconstitutional solely because it results in a racially disproportionate impact. "Disproportionate impact is not irrelevant, but it is not the sole touchstone of an invidious racial discrimination." Proof of racially discriminatory intent or purpose is required to show a violation of the Equal Protection Clause. Although some contrary indications may be drawn from some of our cases, the holding in Davis reaffirmed a principle well established in a variety of contexts.

Davis does not require a plaintiff to prove that the challenged action rested solely on racially discriminatory purposes. Rarely can it be said that a legislature or administrative body operating under a broad mandate made a decision motivated solely by a single concern, or even that a particular purpose was the "dominant" or "primary" one. In fact, it is because legislators and administrators are properly concerned with balancing numerous competing considerations that courts refrain from reviewing the merits of their decisions, absent a showing of arbitrariness or irrationality. But racial discrimination is not just another competing consideration. When there is a proof that a discriminatory purpose has been a motivating factor in the decision, this judicial deference is no longer justified.

Determining Motivating Factors

Determining whether invidious discriminatory purpose was a motivating factor demands a sensitive inquiry into such circumstantial and direct evidence of intent as may be available. The impact of the official action—whether it bears more heavily on one race than another—may provide an important starting point. Sometimes a clear pattern, unexplainable on grounds other than race, emerges from the effect of the state action even when the governing legislation appears neutral on its face. The evidentiary inquiry is then relatively easy. But such cases are rare. Absent a pattern as stark as that in [*Gomillion v. Lightfoot* or *Yick Wo v. Hopkins*], impact alone is not determinative, and the Court must look to other evidence.

The historical background of the decision is one evidentiary source, particularly if it reveals a series of official actions taken for invidious purposes. The specific sequence of events leading up to the challenged decision also may shed some light on the decisionmaker's purposes. For example, if the property involved here always had been zoned R-5 but suddenly was changed to R-3 when the town learned of MHDC's plans to erect integrated housing, we would have a far different case. Departures from the normal procedural sequence also might afford evidence that improper purposes are playing a role. Substantive departures too may be relevant, particularly if the factors usually considered important by the decisionmaker strongly favor a decision contrary to the one reached.

The legislative or administrative history may be highly relevant, especially where there are contemporary statements by members of the decisionmaking body, minutes of its meetings, or reports. In some extraordinary instances the members might be called to the stand at trial to testify concerning the purpose of the official action, although even then such testimony frequently will be barred by privilege.

The foregoing summary identifies, without purporting to be exhaustive, subjects of proper inquiry in determining whether racially discriminatory intent existed. With these in mind, we now address the case before us.

Discriminatory Purpose Must Be Examined

This case was tried in the District Court and reviewed in the Court of Appeals before our decision in *Washington v. Davis*, supra. The respondents proceeded on the erroneous theory that the Village's refusal to rezone carried a racially discriminatory effect and was, without more, unconstitutional. But both courts below understood that at least part of their function was to examine the purpose underlying the decision. In making its findings on this issue, the District Court noted that some of the opponents of Lincoln Green who spoke at the various hearings might have been motivated by opposition to minority groups. The court held, however, that the evidence "does not warrant the conclusion that this motivated the defendants."

On appeal the Court of Appeals focused primarily on respondents' claim that the Village's buffer policy had not been consistently applied and was being invoked with a strictness here that could only demonstrate some other underlying motive. The court concluded that the buffer policy, though not always applied with perfect consistency, had on several occasions formed the basis for the Board's decision to deny other rezoning proposals. "The evidence does not necessitate a finding that Arlington Heights administered this policy in a discriminatory manner." The Court of Appeals therefore approved the District Court's findings concerning the Village's purposes in denying rezoning to MHDC.

Discriminatory Impact Found

We also have reviewed the evidence. The impact of the Village's decision does arguably bear more heavily on racial minorities. Minorities constitute 18% of the Chicago area population, and 40% of the income groups said to be eligible for Lincoln Green. But there is little about the sequence of events leading up to the decision that would spark suspicion. The area around the Viatorian property has been zoned R-3 since 1959, the year when Arlington Heights first adopted a zoning map. Single-family homes surround the 80-acre site, and the Village is undeniably committed to single-family homes as its dominant residential land use. The rezoning request progressed according to the usual procedures. The Plan Commission even scheduled two additional hearings, at least in part to accommodate MHDC and permit it to supplement its presentation with answers to questions generated at the first hearing.

The statements by the Plan Commission and Village Board members, as reflected in the official minutes, focused almost exclusively on the zoning aspects of the MHDC petition, and the zoning factors on which they relied are not novel criteria in the Village's rezoning decisions. There is no reason to doubt that there has been reliance by some neighboring property owners on the maintenance of single-family zoning in the vicinity. The village originally adopted its buffer policy long before MHDC entered the picture and has applied the policy too consistently for us to infer discriminatory purpose from its application in this case. Finally, MHDC called one member of the Village Board to the stand at trial. Nothing in her testimony supports an inference of invidious purpose.

Discriminatory Intent Not Proved

In sum, the evidence does not warrant overturning the concurrent findings of both courts below. Respondents simply failed to carry their burden of proving that discriminatory purpose was a motivating factor in the Village's decision. This conclusion ends the constitutional inquiry. The Court of Appeals' further finding that the Village's decision carried a discriminatory "ultimate effect" is without independent constitutional significance.

"Challenges based upon racial classifications have historically gained the widest judicial acceptance, and it is therefore not surprising that the majority of federal exclusionary zoning cases have focused upon racial concerns."

Racial Discrimination and Zoning Laws

Anonymous

The staff of the Harvard Law Review *reflects Harvard Law School's most esteemed students for the academic year 1977–1978, as well as faculty editors.*

The writer argues that challenges to exclusionary zoning laws often feature the Equal Protection Clause of the Fourteenth Amendment. However, when purposeful discrimination must be proven, success against racial discrimination is difficult to achieve. A number of methods exist to establish racial motive, including evidence of racist statements by the zoning decision makers and those who have influence over the zoning decisions, including the public. The writer concludes that evidence of racial discrimination based on a broad, historical pattern will fail the Arlington Heights *test, which requires evidence of intent. Nevertheless, a claim of discrimination in zoning decisions can succeed if evidence of* specific *racist intent is found.*

"Developments in the Law: Zoning," *Harvard Law Review*, vol. 91, no. 7, May 1978, pp. 1666–1694. Copyright © 1978 The Harvard Law Review Association. Republished with permission of *Harvard Law Review*, conveyed through Copyright Clearance Center, Inc.

72

Once the threshold requirements of justiciability [a concrete dispute between identified parties] have been met, plaintiffs who wish to challenge allegedly exclusionary zoning practices as unconstitutional will ordinarily base their claims upon the equal protection clause of the fourteenth amendment. Equal protection, of course, is more than a convenient doctrinal referent; indeed, its logic suggests both the duty of society and the law to avoid gratuitously imposing stigma and disadvantage upon individuals and the obligation to assure them adequate opportunity to share in the benefits of contemporary life.

Judicial Scrutiny Standards

Yet, because the minimum rationality standard of traditional equal protection law has historically proved to be without significant "bite," plaintiffs in exclusionary zoning cases, attempting to secure closer judicial scrutiny, typically appeal to so-called suspect classifications or fundamental interests. When a state enactment draws upon classifications properly categorized as suspect or somehow impinges upon a fundamental interest, courts will apply strict scrutiny to ensure that the particular enactment is necessary to promote a compelling state interest. In most instances where strict scrutiny is used, courts will be unimpressed with the compelling state interest advanced, and will invalidate the challenged state provision. Challenges based upon racial classifications have historically gained the widest judicial acceptance, and it is therefore not surprising that the majority of federal exclusionary zoning cases have focused upon racial concerns. In the past, however, the precise contours of protection against the use of suspect criteria have been unclear. On the one hand, if equal protection proscribes discriminatory *effects* upon racial groups, then a great number of zoning practices might arguably fall before its imperatives. On the other hand, if only purposeful discriminations are forbidden, then the range of potential strict scrutiny is contracted. The Supreme Court, after suggesting in earlier cases that discriminatory effect is sufficient to trigger equal protection safeguards, held, in *Washington v. Davis*, that racially discriminatory purpose must be shown before a violation is established. In *Village of Arlington Heights v. Metropolitan Housing Development Corp.*, the Supreme Court explicitly applied this test in a zoning context, and concluded that no discriminatory purpose had been proved.

In *Arlington Heights*, a nonprofit corporation sought to build a federally subsidized low-income project in a large, exclusive Chicago suburb. The corporation challenged the town's refusal to permit the desired construction, but the trial court rejected the plaintiff's challenge; it concluded that the town's decision was not discriminatorily motivated and was therefore constitutionally acceptable. The Court of Appeals for the Seventh Circuit reversed, holding that the town's refusal, when interpreted in light of its "historical context and ultimate effect," had a discriminatory impact and thus must be justified by a compelling state interest absent in that case. The Supreme Court reversed and reinstated the trial court's judgment. It held that the constitutional claim must be predicated upon a demonstrated discriminatory purpose, and remanded to the Seventh Circuit for determination of a statutory claim under the Fair Housing Act.

Proving Motive Difficult

While *Arlington Heights* does not require plaintiffs to demonstrate that an illicit purpose was the *primary* impetus for the enactment of a statute challenged as unconstitutional, it does insist that plaintiffs at least point to *an* illicit purpose behind the challenged statute. At first blush, proof of purpose seems an exceedingly difficult task; indeed, the Supreme Court noted in earlier decisions that ascertaining impermissible legislative motive was a prohibitively speculative undertaking. Yet *Arlington Heights*, read together with lower federal court opinions addressing proof requirements in zoning cases, suggests a number of methods by which the requisite purpose may be established.

First, direct proof of subjective discriminatory purpose may be available. While courts cannot expect that decision-makers will frequently furnish a public record of their illicit motives proof of such attitudes may occasionally be inferred from expressions of hostility to the poor or racial minorities in other situations, together with a showing of foreseeable discriminatory effect in the present matter. Second, although it is not dispositive except in extreme cases, the disproportionate impact of a zoning ordinance is an "important starting point" for proof of purpose. Third, courts may infer current discriminatory purpose from a background history of purposeful discriminatory actions. Courts could reject even currently neutral practices which perpetuate the unlawful effects of a prior history of purposeful discrimination. Fourth, the precise sequence of events relevant to a particular decision may be a rich source of evidence of purpose. For example, where a re-zoning to preclude low-income housing is enacted immediately after a specific project is announced, discriminatory purpose may more easily be inferred. Fifth, where the challenged zoning policy is noticeably inconsistent with a locality's past practice, it may reasonably be concluded that some unusual, and perhaps illicit, motive is involved. Finally, the existence of a politically significant, and racially motivated, community group may also encourage a finding of purposeful discrimination. To the extent that a plaintiff can show that there was identifiable private racist activity at the time that the challenged zoning policy was adopted, this evidence can be used to infer that local decisionmakers, presumably highly responsive to the concerns of their constituents, acted impermissibly.

Appropriate Evidence

The precise kinds of proof available in a given instance will depend largely upon the context in which the challenged zoning ordinance was adopted. If the ordinance was adopted pursuant to an administrative action, as in *Arlington Heights*, the methods of proof suggested by the Court in that case are most appropriate. An administrative record will typically be available, thus providing evidence of sequential history and of any direct statements by zoning officials. In addition, past administrative decisions on the record can be compared so as to reveal significant departures in policy. If a public hearing was held, evidence of racial pressure possibly can be obtained. Finally, expert advisory boards may have issued reports whose findings can be used to discount a locality's claim that permissible goals actually lay behind the adoption of a given ordinance.

Specific Intent Required

The conclusion reached in *Arlington Heights*—that evidence grounded in historical context was not, by itself, sufficient to overturn the challenged ordinance—should not be read to preclude plaintiffs from *ever* proving purpose by reference solely to historical context. In *Arlington Heights*, plaintiffs did not point to *specific* purposeful discrimination by the town itself; they merely referred to a broader pattern of discrimination throughout the region, as a result of which Arlington Heights was effectively segregated. Because plantiffs could not demonstrate that the town itself was particularly responsible for purposeful discrimination, the *Arlington Heights* Court was willing to insist that the other objective factors noted above be demonstrated before equal protection liability would attach. Nonetheless, it seems clear that where an historical context involves specific past discriminatory acts by the presently challenged locality, proof of effect alone should provide the court with a sufficiently direct inference of purpose to invalidate the present ordinance.

Many of the objective sources of proof available in the context of administrative action will not be available where the challenged ordinance is the result of a referendum. No record of each voter's motivation exists, and even if a public hearing was held prior to the decision, racist voters need not have voiced their biases loudly or publicly. Even if expert reports were prepared, there is no way to determine whether individual voters were in fact influenced by whatever legitimate concerns those reports might have reflected. In short, courts must give greater weight to remaining factors in deciding challenges both to referenda generally as well as to the results of any particular referendum.

> "[P]olitical support for public housing
> has deteriorated to overt hostility, de-
> spite the staggering need for housing
> assistance today."

Desegregating Public Housing

Cara Hendrickson

*Cara Hendrickson is an associate with the law firm of Kirkland
& Ellis.*

*In the following selection, Hendrickson elucidates that court de-
cisions and Department of Housing and Urban Development
(HUD) regulations pressure affirmative action programs to use
income rather than race to create diversity plans. However, she
posits that income may not reflect race, thereby failing to aid African Americans, who need affirmative action the most. Addressing issues of income does not assist those suffering from current
racial discrimination, nor does it account for the special problems and complex history of race.*

On November 28, 1993, 43-year-old Yetta M. Adams froze
to death on a bench across the street from the Department of Housing and Urban Development ("HUD") in Washington, D.C. According to a childhood friend, Ms. Adams was
a former child care worker, now homeless, who had sought
shelter on that cold night but was turned away. Housing Sec-
retary Cisneros, speaking at Ms. Adams's funeral, said that her
death was a "call to consciousness. . . . She made it clear to
those of us in Government that we must do much better."

Cara Hendrickson, "Racial Desegregation and Income Deconcentration in Public Housing," *Georgetown Journal on Poverty Law & Policy*, vol. IX, no. 1, winter 2002, pp.
35–88. Reproduced by permission.

Housing assistance for the poor has been a contentious topic since its inception in the 1930s. The debate over whether public housing should be reserved for the poorest of the poor or include a range of income groups has plagued the program since its first Congressional realization. In addition, the federal government's complicity in the creation of racially segregated public housing and the subsequent lack of appropriate desegregative responses has created a modern public housing system that is overwhelmingly racially segregated and desperately poor. Further, political support for public housing has deteriorated to overt hostility, despite the staggering need for housing assistance today. . . .

The Current State of Public Housing

The legacy of ambivalence about income requirements and racial segregation is evident in modern public housing. In 1995, there were approximately 1.4 million units of public housing in about 10,000 developments. Many of the residents of public housing developments are desperately poor and overwhelmingly segregated. Despite these conditions, federal aid for housing is in high demand and short supply, and political support for the program is virtually nonexistent.

Today's public housing residents are some of the poorest in history. The median income today for a household in public housing is $5,850, about nineteen percent of the national median income. According to HUD, in 1993, more than eighty percent of non-elderly housing residents across the country live below the poverty line, and most households in large public housing authorities have incomes below twenty percent of the local median.

This poverty is disproportionately borne by African Americans and Hispanics. According to a study published in the *Journal of Urban Affairs* in 1999, twenty-nine percent of African Americans live below the poverty level, while only eight percent of whites do. Although the disparity between the groups varies regionally, in no metropolitan area is the Black poverty rate less than or equal to the white rate. This national situation is amplified in the public housing context, where growing poverty intersects with a legacy of racial segregation. In 1995, two-thirds of all families living in public housing were African American, and one-fifth were Hispanic. Racial minorities living in public housing are even more likely than whites to earn extremely low incomes. Consequently, the effects of poverty in public housing are especially acute for African Americans who reside there. . . .

Persistent Discrimination

Persistent housing discrimination remains an ongoing obstacle to residential integration. According to HUD's Housing Discrimination Survey, African Americans experience racial discrimination approximately fifty-three percent of the time that they visit a rental office to inquire about housing opportunities. The percentage increases for African American homebuyers, who experience discrimination fifty-nine percent of the time they inquire about purchasing a home. "Steering," the practice by which realtors systematically show Black homebuyers houses in neighborhoods that are racially different than those shown to their white counterparts, is also quite common. An African American homebuyer who visits four real estate agents has approximately a forty percent chance of experiencing steering. Further, if an African American renter responds to an advertisement for a unit in an African American neighborhood and the broker has access to other units in predominantly white neighborhoods, the broker will withhold this information from the renters eighty percent of the time. As Lance Freeman wrote, "If African Americans were able to exercise their preferences and receive returns to their individual traits in a manner similar to Asians or Latinos, residential segregation would be at much lower rates than currently reported." From this evidence, it is clear that residential segregation disproportionately burdens African Americans and is critically linked to race.

Scarcity and Political Unpopularity

Increased poverty, as well as decreased political support for public housing, has led to a high demand for public housing that is largely unmet. The relatively modest increases in the number of vouchers and units provided has not come close to meeting the need for affordable housing units. Between 1970 and 1995, the number of low-income renters increased seventy percent, but the total number of units available to low-income renters has fallen. Today, although 15 million households qualify for federal housing assistance, only 4.5 million actually receive aid. Of the more than 10 million who do not receive federal assistance, HUD estimates that more than half have "worst case" housing problems, paying more than half of their incomes for housing or living in seriously substandard apartments.

As a result, there are over 900,000 families on waiting lists for public housing units, and about 1.4 million waiting for housing subsidies. For them, the average time spent waiting for a housing voucher is over two years. The wait is even greater in areas with large public housing authorities; the wait is now, on average, five years in Chicago, eight years in New York, and ten years in Los Angeles.

At the same time that the demand for federal public housing assistance is at an all-time high, political support for the programs is almost non-existent. HUD programs have been de-funded, disavowed, and threatened with abolishment. In the midst of the 1994 elections, then-House Speaker Newt Gingrich claimed, "You could abolish HUD tomorrow morning and improve life in most of America." In May of 1995, Congress rescinded $6.3 billion that had already been authorized for the HUD budget for Fiscal Year 1995. This cut one-quarter of the agency's budget, mostly in the areas of funds for existing public housing projects and Section 8 subsidized developments. The Fiscal Year 1996 budget, providing $19 billion for HUD, was a reduction of more than one-quarter of its budget. Many believed this budget reduction to be part of an eventual elimination of the agency.

Political Hostility

This political hostility is directed at public housing programs in particular; other forms of federal housing assistance flourish. The government spends four times as much on mortgage interest and property tax deductions ($66 billion a year) as it does on low-income housing (approximately $26 billion); more than two-thirds of the funds for these programs go to families with incomes over $75,000. At the same time that many renters are finding it extremely difficult to meet their monthly rent obligations, homeowners have seen their mortgages consume an ever-smaller portion of their after-tax income.

In 1994, reacting to antagonism from Congress, HUD proposed its "Blueprint for Change" to ward off proposals to abolish HUD or eliminate housing programs. The Blueprint proposed by HUD would have dismantled federal public housing assistance as it is known today, replacing Section 8 vouchers and public housing with block grants to states for housing assistance. Although the Blueprint was never implemented in its proposed form, the assault on public housing programs has not abated. In both 1997 and 1998, Congress imposed freezes on the creation of new vouchers. Despite the fact that the years 1999 and 2000 saw modest increases in the number of new vouchers created, prospects for growth of the public housing program under a new Republican administration are grim.

> "Decades after the enactment of reason-
> ably strong legal prohibitions against
> racial discrimination and segregation
> in housing, pervasive racial discrimina-
> tion and segregation in federally as-
> sisted and other housing still exists."

Discrimination and Segregation in Federal Housing

Florence Wagman Roisman

*Florence Wagman Roisman is a law professor at Indiana Univer-
sity School of Law—Indianapolis.*

*In the following selection, Roisman reveals that despite Supreme
Court restrictions on the reach of civil rights laws regarding
housing such as those discussed in* Arlington Heights, *the Court
has not overruled early decisions. Consequently, the Court continues to stress the importance of fair housing. She suggests that
because Congress and the presidency are showing decreased interest in civil rights, fair housing must be assured and promoted
through litigation.*

This Article considers a paradox: although Title VI of the
1964 Civil Rights Act and related legal standards prohibit
racial discrimination in federally assisted housing programs,
pervasive racial discrimination and segregation still character-
ize those programs in 2005. . . .

Florence Wagman Roisman, "Keeping the Promise: Ending Racial Discrimination and
Segregation in Federally Financed Housing," *Howard Law Journal*, vol. 48, no. 3,
spring 2005, pp. 913–36. Copyright © 2005 by the Howard University School of Law.
Reproduced by permission.

Federal Laws

Standing alone, Title VI of the 1964 Civil Rights Act was not an effective interdiction of racial discrimination and segregation. Unlike its precursor, President Kennedy's 1962 Executive Order 11,063, Title VI did not apply to the Federal Housing Administration (FHA) and Veterans Administration (VA) home ownership programs, and did not explicitly require correction of past discrimination or segregation. Soon thereafter, however, legislation, regulations, and judicial decisions governing racial discrimination and segregation in federally assisted housing became much more strict and comprehensive. Title VIII of the 1968 Civil Rights Act forbade racial discrimination in almost all housing units in the United States, and directed that all federal agencies "shall" administer their housing programs "in a manner affirmatively to further" fair housing policies. The 1988 Fair Housing Amendments Act substantially strengthened the 1968 Act, and various housing and community development statutes later explicitly extended the "affirmatively to further" and related obligations to public housing authorities and other agencies.

With respect to administrative implementation, the Department of Housing and Urban Development (HUD) promulgated regulations that enhanced the power of the legislation, notably by prohibiting actions that have the effect of discriminating on the basis of race and by requiring actions that would undo the effects of past discrimination.

Court Decisions

Early court decisions also helped to attack racial discrimination and segregation in housing. In the 1960s and 1970s, the Supreme Court held that the 1866 Civil Rights Act applied to private discrimination in housing and encouraged broad interpretations of Title VIII with respect to coverage, standing, and reading the statute as banning segregation as well as discrimination. Although the Supreme Court later restricted the breadth of the housing civil rights laws, holding that intentional discrimination was needed to establish a claim under the 1866 Act, Title VI, and the Constitution [*Village of Arlington Heights v. Metropolitan Housing Development Corporation*], it has allowed disparate impact as a basis for liability under Title VIII, not rejecting the lower courts' decisions following *Griggs v. Duke Power Co.* in this regard. More recently, the Supreme Court has refused to allow private enforcement of the Title VI disparate impact regulations, and, although it has not yet invalidated those regulations, it certainly seems to have signaled the likelihood that it will do so. The Supreme Court has not, however, overruled its earlier decisions emphasizing the importance of fair housing; indeed, it recently has agreed that fair housing is an "overriding societal priority." Thus, taking into account a mixed record with respect to judicial decisions, overall the law-making and law-interpreting institutions have taken a strong stand against racial discrimination and segregation in federally assisted housing and, indeed, in all housing.

The crucial point, however, is that none of this lawmaking and law interpreting has had significant impact in the "real world." All housing in the United States is characterized by pervasive racial discrimination and segregation: the 2000 Housing Discrimination Study showed continuing, substantial discrimination against Blacks and Hispanics in the rental and sale of housing and the 2000 Census demonstrated that, while residential racial segregation of Blacks has been declining slightly, it still is at such high levels that if it continued to decline at the same rate, it would be decades before a moderate level of segregation were reached. With respect to what should have been the easiest venue in which to end racial discrimination and segregation—housing assisted by the federal government—the sad, shameful fact is that, despite all these statutes and regulations and judicial decisions, the federal government is still—forty years after the 1964 Civil Rights Act—spending billions of dollars to keep people of color in housing that is separate and unequal, in units, buildings, and neighborhoods that are vastly inferior to the units and buildings and neighborhoods in which federal housing dollars help white, "Anglo" people to live. . . .

Keeping the Promise

Decades after the enactment of reasonably strong legal prohibitions against racial discrimination and segregation in housing, pervasive racial discrimination and segregation in federally assisted and other housing still exists. This shows that what we have been doing with respect to Title VI (and Title VIII) enforcement has not been working very effectively, and we need to do something different.

Certainly, civil rights advocates should consider how federal legislative and agency enforcement could be improved, though the next few years do not seem likely to present good opportunities for such changes. But civil rights supporters will have to respond to the proposals of others, in Congress and in the agencies, and should, in any event, always be planning for the future. Proponents of civil rights should develop federal legislative and administrative proposals designed to improve fair housing enforcement.

With respect to Title VIII in general, this discussion has begun. Relatively little creative thinking, however, has been addressed to the specific problem of ending and undoing the effects of discrimination and segregation in the federally financed housing programs. Calls for improved Title VI enforcement have not been effective; depending upon HUD to undo the derelictions in HUD's own programs has been shown to be unrealistic. Creative and thoughtful proposals certainly should be developed for ending governmental complicity in discrimination and segregation.

Possible Solutions

In addition to developing new federal legislative and administrative proposals, advocates should attend immediately and thoroughly to housing/civil rights issues at the state and local levels. It would be helpful to encourage the enactment and enforcement of inclusionary zoning ordinances and statutes, of legislation that preserves units threatened with loss and prevents displacement, and of state and local fair housing laws that eliminate exemptions, improve enforcement, and extend protections by prohibiting discrimination on the bases of source of income, age, marital status, sexual orientation, and other characteristics not protected by federal law.

Furthermore, there is much room for improvement in enforcement of existing legal requirements. HUD—and Department of Agriculture—financed projects, for example, are required to have Affirmative Fair Housing Marketing Plans, but often do not have or do not follow those plans. Fair housing and mobility groups should insist on enforcement of the affirmative marketing requirements. With respect to the Housing Choice Voucher Program, advocates should encourage mobility counseling, vastly improved landlord recruitment and PHA administration, and regional administration. . . .

The Importance of Litigation

If any lesson is to be learned from recent history, it is that the one tool that has been effective in ameliorating racial discrimination and segregation in federally assisted housing has been litigation. As Congress and the executive branch have become substantially less interested in civil rights, litigation seems even more important than it has been in the past. To be sure, the courts are becoming more conservative, but litigation on these issues still is reasonably likely to succeed, because the underlying, substantive legal standards are so strong. Much of the negative decision-making in the federal courts has been with respect to doctrines that prevent or delay reaching the merits—such as restrictions with respect to standing [right to sure] and causes of action [specific claims]. What advocates need to do is to be strategic and thorough. By strategic, I mean that we need to think hard about how to use limited litigation and research resources, and select lawsuits that will make the most impact and bring them in courts—state as well as federal—that are likely to give them fair consideration. By thorough, I mean that the records of intentional discrimination and segregation need to be made. Two outstanding civil rights litigators told us years ago that intentional racial discrimination almost always can be found if one looks for it. I think we need to spend energy making those records.

CHAPTER 3

Employment

Case Overview

Adarand Constructors, Inc. v. Pena (1995)

The Supreme Court confirmed that all racial preferences imposed by any local, state, or federal government must be examined by a reviewing court under strict scrutiny. In this case, a subcontractor, Adarand Constructors, disputed a federal agency contract clause that provides a financial incentive to contractors who hire disadvantaged subcontractors. Adarand submitted the lowest bid on a highway construction contract, but the contract was awarded to a minority subcontractor. Adarand sued, arguing that race-based presumptions contained in subcontractor compensation clauses violated the Equal Protection Clause of the Fifth Amendment's Due Process Clause. The district court and court of appeals upheld the contractor clause, citing the intermediate scrutiny standards of *Fullilove v. Klutznick* (1980) and *Metro Broadcasting, Inc. v. FCC* (1990).

Justice Sandra Day O'Connor, in the majority opinion, ruled that all race-based actions by a government must be subjected to strict scrutiny, thus overruling the intermediate level of review in *Fullilove* and *Metro Broadcasting*. The Court opined that a reviewing court must be skeptical of racial classifications. Courts must also consider that the individuals receiving unequal treatment under a race-based action have the right to demand a strict judicial review of the harming law. The high level of review must determine whether a racial preference is benign and legitimate. In addition, a racial group classification must not infringe upon an individual's right to equal protection under both the Fifth and Fourteenth Amendments.

All governmental race-based actions must serve a compelling interest, and must be narrowly tailored to serve that interest. Strict scrutiny, Justice O'Connor asserted, is the best means to ensure thorough examination of racial classifications. Although the level of scrutiny is detailed and rigorous, it does not signify that all racial preferences will be found invalid. Some race-based actions will satisfy a compelling governmental interest if they are precise and narrowly tailored.

In the *Adarand* decision, the Court recognized that racial discrimination continues in this country and that the government must be allowed to address the lingering effects of racial discrimination. Prior to 1964, especially in the South, many factories and businesses exercised clearly discriminatory policies against minorities. After passage of the Civil Rights Act, most companies worked to comply with the law; however, the remnants of past discrimination carried forward. Therefore, courts and legislators deemed it necessary to strike down racially neutral laws and impose corrective laws which became known as affirmative action. *Adarand* affirmed the need for close examination of affirmative-action practices to verify that a policy or program is benign, legitimate, and not unduly burdensome to the historically favored race.

> "'[A] free people whose institutions are founded upon the doctrine of equality,' should tolerate no retreat from the principle that government may treat people differently because of their race only for the most compelling reasons."

The Court's Decision: Racial Classifications Must Serve a Compelling Governmental Interest

Sandra Day O'Connor

Sandra Day O'Connor, the first woman on the U.S. Supreme Court, was nominated to the Court by President Reagan in 1981. She served on the Court until 2006.

Justice Sandra Day O'Connor, in her majority opinion regarding the rights of a non-minority subcontractor, ruled that all racial classifications imposed by any government must be analyzed by a reviewing court under strict scrutiny. Such level of scrutiny of race-based classifications is required to determine whether a racial preference is benign. Since both the Fifth and Fourteenth Amendments protect persons, not groups, any race-based governmental action, she declares, should be held to detailed judicial inquiry to verify that the personal right to equal protection has not been violated. In addition, Justice O'Connor concludes that state and federal racial classifications must serve a compelling governmental interest and must be narrowly tailored to further that interest.

Sandra Day O'Connor, majority opinion, *Adarand Constructors, Inc. v. Pena*, 515 U.S. 200, 1995.

Petitioner Adarand Constructors, Inc., claims that the Federal Government's practice of giving general contractors on government projects a financial incentive to hire subcontractors controlled by "socially and economically disadvantaged individuals," and in particular, the Government's use of race-based presumptions in identifying such individuals, violates the equal protection component of the Fifth Amendment's Due Process Clause. . . .

What Is the Required Level of Scrutiny?

With [*Richmond v. J.A. Croson Co.* (1989)], the Court finally agreed that the Fourteenth Amendment requires strict scrutiny of all race-based action by state and local governments. But *Croson* of course had no occasion to declare what standard of review the Fifth Amendment requires for such action taken by the Federal Government. . . .

Despite lingering uncertainty in the details, however, the Court's cases through *Croson* had established three general propositions with respect to governmental racial classifications. First, skepticism: [a]ny preference based on racial or ethnic criteria must necessarily receive a most searching examination. Second, consistency: the standard of review under the Equal Protection Clause is not dependent on the race of those burdened or benefited by a particular classification. And third, congruence: [e]qual protection analysis in the Fifth Amendment area is the same as that under the Fourteenth Amendment. Taken together, these three propositions lead to the conclusion that any person of whatever race, has the right to demand that any governmental actor subject to the Constitution justify any racial classification subjecting that person to unequal treatment under the strictest judicial scrutiny. . . .

Is the Classification Benign?

A year later, however, the Court took a surprising turn. *Metro Broadcasting, Inc. v. FCC* (1990), involved a Fifth Amendment challenge to two race-based policies of the Federal Communications Commission. In *Metro Broadcasting*, the Court repudiated the long-held notion that "it would be unthinkable that the same Constitution would impose a lesser duty on the Federal Government" than it does on a State to afford equal protection of the laws. It did so by holding that "benign" federal racial classifications need only satisfy intermediate scrutiny, even though *Croson* had recently concluded that such classifications enacted by a State must satisfy strict scrutiny. "[B]enign" federal racial classifications, the Court said, "—even if those measures are not 'remedial' in the sense of being designed to compensate victims of past governmental or societal discrimination—are constitutionally permissible to the extent that they serve important governmental objectives within the power of Congress and are substantially related to achievement of those objectives." The Court did not explain how to tell whether a racial classification should be deemed "benign," other than to express "confiden[ce] that an 'examination of the legislative scheme and its history' will separate benign measures from other types of racial classifications."

Applying this test, the Court first noted that the FCC policies at issue did not serve as a remedy for past discrimination. Proceeding on the assumption that the policies were nonetheless "benign," it concluded that they served the "important governmental objective" of "enhancing broadcast diversity," and that they were "substantially related" to that objective. It therefore upheld the policies.

By adopting intermediate scrutiny as the standard of review for congressionally mandated "benign" racial classifications, *Metro Broadcasting* departed from prior cases in two significant respects. First, it turned its back on *Croson*'s explanation of why strict scrutiny of all governmental racial classifications is essential:

"Absent searching judicial inquiry into the justification for such race-based measures, there is simply no way of determining what classifications are 'benign' or 'remedial' and what classifications are in fact motivated by illegitimate notions of racial inferiority or simple racial politics. Indeed, the purpose of strict scrutiny is to 'smoke out' illegitimate uses of race by assuring that the legislative body is pursuing a goal important enough to warrant use of a highly suspect tool. The test also ensures that the means chosen 'fit' this compelling goal so closely that there is little or no possibility that the motive for the classification was illegitimate racial prejudice or stereotype."

We adhere to that view today, despite the surface appeal of holding "benign" racial classifications to a lower standard, because it may not always be clear that a so-called preference is in fact benign. "[M]ore than good motives should be required when government seeks to allocate its resources by way of an explicit racial classification system."

Second, *Metro Broadcasting* squarely rejected one of the three propositions established by the Court's earlier equal protection cases, namely, congruence between the standards applicable to federal and state racial classifications, and in so doing also undermined the other two skepticisms of all racial classifications, and consistency of treatment irrespective of the race of the burdened or benefited group. Under *Metro Broadcasting*, certain racial classifications ("benign" ones enacted by the Federal Government) should be treated less skeptically than others; and the race of the benefited group is critical to the determination of which standard of review to apply. *Metro Broadcasting* was thus a significant departure from much of what had come before it.

Are Personal Rights Protected?

The three propositions undermined by *Metro Broadcasting* all derive from the basic principle that the Fifth and Fourteenth Amendments to the Constitution protect persons, not groups. It follows from that principle that all governmental action based on race—a group classification long recognized as "in most circumstances irrelevant and therefore prohibited,"—

should be subjected to detailed judicial inquiry to ensure that the personal right to equal protection of the laws has not been infringed. These ideas have long been central to this Court's understanding of equal protection, and holding "benign" state and federal racial classifications to different standards does not square with them. "[A] free people whose institutions are founded upon the doctrine of equality," should tolerate no retreat from the principle that government may treat people differently because of their race only for the most compelling reasons. Accordingly, we hold today that all racial classifications, imposed by whatever federal, state, or local governmental actor, must be analyzed by a reviewing court under strict scrutiny. In other words, such classifications are constitutional only if they are narrowly tailored measures that further compelling governmental interests. To the extent that *Metro Broadcasting* is inconsistent with that holding, it is overruled. . . .

Are the Classifications Compelling and Narrowly Tailored?

Our action today makes explicit what Justice Powell thought implicit in the *Fullilove* lead opinion: federal racial classifications, like those of a State, must serve a compelling governmental interest, and must be narrowly tailored to further that interest. Of course, it follows that to the extent (if any) that *Fullilove* held federal racial classifications to be subject to a less rigorous standard, it is no longer controlling. But we need not decide today whether the program upheld in *Fullilove* would survive strict scrutiny as our more recent cases have defined it.

Some have questioned the importance of debating the proper standard of review of race-based legislation. But we agree with Justice Stevens that "[b]ecause racial characteristics so seldom provide a relevant basis for disparate treatment, and because classifications based on race are potentially so harmful to the entire body politic, it is especially important that the reasons for any such classification be clearly identified and unquestionably legitimate," and that "[r]acial classifications are simply too pernicious to permit any but the most exact connection between justification and classification." We think that requiring strict scrutiny is the best way to ensure that courts will consistently give racial classifications that kind of detailed examination, both as to ends and as to means. . . .

Finally, we wish to dispel the notion that strict scrutiny is strict in theory, but fatal in fact. The unhappy persistence of both the practice and the lingering effects of racial discrimination against minority groups in this country is an unfortunate reality, and government is not disqualified from acting in response to it. As recently as 1987, for example, every Justice of this Court agreed that the Alabama Department of Public Safety's "pervasive, systematic, and obstinate discriminatory conduct" justified a narrowly tailored race-based remedy. When race-based action is necessary to further a compelling interest, such action is within constitutional constraints if it satisfies the "narrow tailoring" test this Court has set out in previous cases.

> "[T]here are circumstances in which Government may, consistently with the Constitution, adopt programs aimed at remedying the effects of past invidious discrimination."

Dissenting Opinion: Equal Protection under the Fourteenth Amendment Satisfies the Strict Scrutiny Test

David H. Souter

David H. Souter began his tenure on the Supreme Court in 1990, upon his appointment to the bench by President George H. W. Bush.

Justice Souter, in his dissenting opinion, asserts that prior cases applying intermediate scrutiny to affirmative-action disputes should dictate the standard of review. Justice Souter opines that the Equal Protection Clause of the Fourteenth Amendment is broad enough and important enough to satisfy the strict scrutiny test the majority opinion seeks to apply. Not only does the government have the power to issue a decree eliminating the discriminatory effects of the past, it also has the power and duty to act to prevent future discrimination. Accordingly, in its effort to remedy past racial discrimination, the government may impose a race-based action that harms the traditionally favored race. Such harm is acceptable, he argues, if it is both reasonable and temporary.

David H. Souter, dissenting opinion, *Adarand Constructors, Inc. v. Pena*, 515 U.S. 200, 1995.

The Court today ... does not reach the application of *Fullilove* [*Fullilove v. Klutznick* (1980)—intermediate scrutiny] to the facts of this case, and on remand it will be incumbent on the Government and petitioner to address anew the facts upon which statutes like these must be judged on the Government's remedial theory of justification: facts about the current effects of past discrimination, the necessity for a preferential remedy, and the suitability of this particular preferential scheme. Petitioner could, of course, have raised all of these issues under the standard employed by the *Fullilove* plurality, and without now trying to read the current congressional evidentiary record that may bear on resolving these issues I have to recognize the possibility that proof of changed facts might have rendered *Fullilove*'s conclusion obsolete as judged under the *Fullilove* plurality's own standard. Be that as it may, it seems fair to ask whether the statutes will meet a different fate from what *Fullilove* would have decreed. The answer is, quite probably not, though of course there will be some interpretive forks in the road before the significance of strict scrutiny for congressional remedial statutes becomes entirely clear.

Reach of Fourteenth Amendment Unclear

In assessing the degree to which today's holding portends a departure from past practice, it is also worth noting that nothing in today's opinion implies any view of Congress's §5 power and the deference due its exercise that differs from the views expressed by the *Fullilove* plurality. The Court simply notes the observation in *Croson* [*Richmond v. J.A. Croson Co.* (1989)] "that the Court's 'treatment of an exercise of congressional power in *Fullilove* cannot be dispositive here,' because *Croson*'s facts did not implicate Congress' broad power under 5 of the Fourteenth Amendment," and explains that there is disagreement among today's majority about the extent of the §5 power. There is therefore no reason to treat the opinion as affecting one way or another the views of §5 power, described as "broad," "unique," and "unlike [that of] any state or political subdivision," *Croson*. Thus, today's decision should leave §5 exactly where it is as the source of an interest of the national government sufficiently important to satisfy the corresponding requirement of the strict scrutiny test.

Racial Classifications May Remedy Past Discrimination

Finally, I should say that I do not understand that today's decision will necessarily have any effect on the resolution of an issue that was just as pertinent under *Fullilove*'s unlabeled standard as it is under the standard of strict scrutiny now adopted by the Court. The Court has long accepted the view that constitutional authority to remedy past discrimination is not limited to the power to forbid its continuation, but extends to eliminating those effects that would otherwise persist and skew the operation of public systems even in the absence of current intent to practice any discrimination. Indeed, a majority of the Court today reiterates that there are circumstances in which Government may, consistently with the Constitution, adopt programs aimed at remedying the effects of past invidious discrimination.

Remedial Mechanism May Harm the Favored Race

When the extirpation [extermination] of lingering discriminatory effects is thought to require a catch-up mechanism, like the racially preferential inducement under the statutes considered here, the result may be that some members of the historically favored race are hurt by that remedial mechanism, however innocent they may be of any personal responsibility for any discriminatory conduct. When this price is considered reasonable, it is in part because it is a price to be paid only temporarily; if the justification for the preference is eliminating the effects of a past practice, the assumption is that the effects will themselves recede into the past, becoming attenuated and finally disappearing. Thus, Justice Powell wrote in his concurring opinion in *Fullilove* that the "temporary nature of this remedy ensures that a race-conscious program will not last longer than the discriminatory effects it is designed to eliminate."

Surely the transition from the *Fullilove* plurality view (in which Justice Powell joined) to today's strict scrutiny (which will presumably be applied as Justice Powell employed it) does not signal a change in the standard by which the burden of a remedial racial preference is to be judged as reasonable or not at any given time.

> "[A] carefully designed affirmative ac-
> tion program may help to realize, fi-
> nally, the 'equal protection of the laws'
> the Fourteenth Amendment has prom-
> ised since 1868."

Dissenting Opinion: Strict Scrutiny Must Not Conflict with the Equal Protection Clause

Ruth Bader Ginsburg

Ruth Bader Ginsburg, as a law professor at Rutgers University, helped to write the brief for the historic Supreme Court case on gender discrimination, Reed v. Reed, *in 1971. She was appointed to the Supreme Court in 1993.*

Justice Ginsburg, in her dissenting opinion, acknowledges that the Court seeks to distinguish legitimate from illegitimate race-based classifications and to determine benign from malign affirmative action programs. While Justice Ginsburg agrees that close review is warranted, she believes that the strict scrutiny standard will prevent even benign racial classifications from surviving. She highlights the role of Congress in its authority to remedy past racial discrimination and review its existing race-based programs. Justice Ginsburg ends her dissent with the hope that the majority decision is one that will evolve according to the changing conditions of society.

Ruth Bader Ginsburg, dissenting opinion, *Adarand Constructors, Inc. v. Pena*, 515 U.S 200, 1995.

For the reasons stated by Justice Souter, and in view of the attention the political branches are currently giving the matter of affirmative action, I see no compelling cause for the intervention the Court has made in this case. I further agree with Justice Stevens that, in this area, large deference is owed by the Judiciary to "Congress' institutional competence and constitutional authority to overcome historic racial subjugation."

Racial Discrimination Continues

The statutes and regulations at issue, as the Court indicates, were adopted by the political branches in response to an "unfortunate reality": "[t]he unhappy persistence of both the practice and the lingering effects of racial discrimination against minority groups in this country." The United States suffers from those lingering effects because, for most of our Nation's history, the idea that "we are just one race" (Scalia, J., concurring in part and concurring in judgement) was not embraced. For generations, our lawmakers and judges were unprepared to say that there is in this land no superior race, no race inferior to any other. In *Plessy v. Ferguson* (1896), not only did this Court endorse the oppressive practice of race segregation, but even Justice Harlan, the advocate of a "colorblind" Constitution, stated:

> "The white race deems itself to be the dominant race in this country. And so it is, in prestige, in achievements, in education, in wealth and in power. So, I doubt not, it will continue to be for all time, if it remains true to its great heritage and holds fast to the principles of constitutional liberty."

Not until *Loving v. Virginia* (1967), which held unconstitutional Virginia's ban on interracial marriages, could one say with security that the Constitution and this Court would abide no measure "designed to maintain White Supremacy."

The divisions in this difficult case should not obscure the Court's recognition of the persistence of racial inequality and a majority's acknowledgement of Congress' authority to act affirmatively, not only to end discrimination, but also to counteract discrimination's lingering effects. Those effects, reflective of a system of racial caste only recently ended, are evident in our workplaces, markets, and neighborhoods. Job applicants with identical resumes, qualifications, and interview styles still experience different receptions, depending on their race. White and African-American consumers still encounter different deals. People of color looking for housing still face discriminatory treatment by landlords, real estate agents, and mortgage lenders. Minority entrepreneurs sometimes fail to gain contracts though they are the low bidders, and they are sometimes refused work even after winning contracts. Bias both conscious and unconscious, reflecting traditional and unexamined habits of thought, keeps up barriers that must come down if equal opportunity and nondiscrimination are ever genuinely to become this country's law and practice.

Given this history and its practical consequences, Congress surely can conclude that a carefully designed affirmative action program may help to realize, finally, the "equal protection of the laws" the Fourteenth Amendment has promised since 1868.

Strict Scrunity Will Prevent Remedies for Racial Discrimination

The lead opinion uses one term, "strict scrutiny," to describe the standard of judicial review for all governmental classifications by race. But that opinion's elaboration strongly suggests that the strict standard announced is indeed "fatal" for classifications burdening groups that have suffered discrimination in our society. That seems to me, and, I believe, to the Court, the enduring lesson one should draw from *Korematsu v. United States* (1944); for in that case, scrutiny the Court described as "most rigid," nonetheless yielded a pass for an odious, gravely injurious racial classification. A *Korematsu*-type classification, as I read the opinions in this case, will never again survive scrutiny: such a classification, history and precedent instruct, properly ranks as prohibited.

Close Review Appropriate

Properly, a majority of the Court calls for review that is searching, in order to ferret out classifications in reality malign, but masquerading as benign. The Court's once lax review of sex-based classifications demonstrates the need for such suspicion. Today's decision thus usefully reiterates that the purpose of strict scrutiny "is precisely to distinguish legitimate from illegitimate uses of race in governmental decisionmaking," "to 'differentiate between' permissible and impermissible governmental use of race."

Close review also is in order for this further reason. As Justice Souter points out (dissenting opinion), and as this very case shows, some members of the historically favored race can be hurt by catch-up mechanisms designed to cope with the lingering effects of entrenched racial subjugation. Court review can ensure that preferences are not so large as to trammel unduly upon the opportunities of others or interfere too harshly with legitimate expectations of persons in once-preferred groups.

While I would not disturb the programs challenged in this case, and would leave their improvement to the political branches, I see today's decision as one that allows our precedent to evolve, still to be informed by and responsive to changing conditions.

> "[I]f our interest is achieving a just so-
> ciety, then there is nothing in the sorry
> history of affirmative action abuses that
> requires us to tie our hands with a
> color-blind formalism."

The Pros and Cons
of Affirmative Action

Glenn C. Loury

*Glenn C. Loury is a professor of economics and director of the
Institute on Race and Social Division at Boston University.*

*Many argue that people should be valued as individuals, regard-
less of race and gender. In the following selection, Loury asserts
that race is a significant identity trait and an important means
of identifying inequitable business practices. He also underscores
that social networks are influenced by race, thereby inevitably
limiting or enhancing employment and social opportunities.
Therefore the government cannot achieve social goals through
"color-blind" treatment of its citizens.*

The issue of Affirmative Action is discussed, identifying
some difficulties with the way that this policy has been
pursued in the past: Racial preferences can be a poorly targeted method of closing the gap in social status between Blacks
and Whites, and can have negative, unintended consequences
for incentives and for the reputations of its beneficiaries. . . .

Non-Discrimination Principle

Of course it is a basic principle of political liberalism—sometimes called the "non-discrimination principle"—that per-

Glenn C. Loury, "Who Cares about Racial Inequality?" *Journal of Sociology & Social
Welfare*, vol. 27, no. 1, March 2000, pp. 133–51. Reproduced by permission.

sonal characteristics like race, sex, and ethnicity should have no moral relevance. People are to be valued as individuals, not as the representatives of groups. In the economic theory of social choice, for example, this idea is captured by the concept of "anonymity": the idea that the legitimacy of any given government benefit depends upon the fact that it is distributed without regard to the identities, as distinct from the conditions, of those who get the benefit and those who do not. This is the ideal. . . .

Why Care about Racial Inequality?

Thus, we arrive at the fundament question: Why should we care about racial inequality per se? What is wrong with a situation in which blacks are roughly 12 percent of the U.S. population, but some 40 percent of welfare recipients, 50 percent of incarcerated felons, and 3 percent of newly graduating engineers? Why should we care about the racial composition of the police forces in large cities, of Presidential appointees to the federal bench, or of the freshman class at a state university? Why should a large corporation actively seek a qualified black candidate for a position in its upper management? After all, thinking in the abstract, a growing welfare population or an increasing number of incarcerated felons is a problem for society no matter what the color of those citizens. What matters is that we reduce the total numbers, right?

Actually, I will argue that this is not right, or at least not for America, not today. A President who appoints hundreds of local federal judges among whom there are no blacks invites a wholly unnecessary political firestorm. He would rightly find himself in trouble. A corporation that neglects to bring along some blacks into upper management exposes itself needlessly to potential difficulties with its customers or its lower-level employees. A racially diverse big city fielding a nearly all white police force is asking for big trouble the next time a drunken black motorist has to be forcibly subdued. A freshman class devoid of blacks teaches it students some lessons about our society that are not listed in the course catalog. And to accept with equanimity the blackening of our prisons or welfare rolls is to be indifferent, I suggest, to an important aspect of social justice.

Reasons to Care: Personal Identity

One reason to care about racial inequality is that race forms an important part of the personal identity of many citizens. Ideally, these racial identities should be irrelevant to our dealings with one another. Yet clearly they are not. As a result, all kinds of circumstances, having nothing to do with "racial preferences," require a government to depart from the strictly "color-blind" treatment of its citizens in order to discharge its legitimate function. . . .

Reasons to Care: Racial Information

Another reason to care about racial inequality is that race is an important source of information in many situations. Race is an easily observable trait that, as an empirical matter, is correlated with some hard-to-observe traits about which employers, lenders, police officers and others are concerned. Direct evidence from employer interviews indicates that both black and white employers are reluctant to hire black, urban young males who exhibit lower-class behavioral styles. Racial identity is also used as information in a variety of ways by police. Some evidence indicates that it shapes their law enforcement decisions. Indeed, the dramatic disparity between the races in the rates of arrest and incarceration for criminal offenses must be taken into account when discussing racial differences in the labor market experiences of males, though the direction of causality is difficult to untangle. . . .

Reasons to Care: Social Networks

Yet another reason to care about racial inequality is that race influences the social networks that are open to individuals, and these networks in turn have a major effect upon individuals' opportunities. Here are two observations that illustrate the key to my argument: First, all societies exhibit significant social segmentation. People make choices about whom to befriend, whom to marry, where to live, to which schools to send their children and so on. Factors like race, ethnicity, social class, and religious affiliation influence these choices of association. Second, the processes through which individuals develop their productive capacities are shaped by custom, convention, and social norms, and are not fully responsive to market forces, or reflective of the innate abilities of persons. Networks of social affiliation are not usually the result of calculated economic decisions. They nevertheless help determine how resources important to the development of the productive capacities of human beings are made available to individuals. . . .

Are Affirmative Action Polices Necessary?

This argument leads naturally to the question of whether affirmative-action policies are necessary and justified. To emphasize that racial group disparities can be transmitted across generations through subtle and complex social processes is not necessarily to endorse employment or educational preferences based on race. But recognizing the importance of social segmentation does cause one to doubt the ethical viability, and indeed the logical coherence, of "color-blind absolutism"—the notion that the Constitution requires government agents to ignore the racial identity of citizens. Ironically, recent claims by some conservatives to this effect bear an eerie resemblance, in form and in substance, to the similarly absolute claims of some card-carrying civil libertarians on behalf of a "wall of separation" between church and state.

Consider that, as a practical matter, the government cannot enforce laws against employment discrimination without taking note of a gross demographic imbalance in an employer's work force. Yet, the government's requiring that employment data be reported by race is already a departure from pure color-blind behavior. So too is the practice, nearly universal in the public and private sectors, of targeted outreach efforts designed to increase the representation of blacks in the pool of persons considered for an employment opportunity. Accordingly, the more intellectually consistent of the color-blind absolutists now recommend, as logic would require, that we repeal the civil-rights laws and abandon even those efforts to achieve racial diversity which do not involve preferential treatment. But is that stance consistent with fairness?

Coming up with cases that challenge the absolutist claim is not difficult. How can a college educator convey to students the lesson that "not all blacks think alike," with too few blacks on campus for this truth to be evident? Can the police consider race when making undercover assignments? Can a black public employee use health insurance benefits to choose a black therapist with whom to discuss race-related anxieties? Can units in a public housing project be let with an eye to sustaining a racially integrated environment? What about a National Science Foundation that encourages gifted blacks to pursue careers in the fields where few now study? Clearly, there is no general rule that can resolve all of these cases reasonably.

Costs of Racial Preferences

I want to be clear. This criticism of color-blind absolutism is not an unqualified defense of the affirmative action status quo. There are many reasons to suspect that in particular contexts the costs of using racial preferences will outweigh the benefits. One such reason for questioning the wisdom of affirmative action in certain contexts is that the widespread use of preference can logically be expected to erode the perception of black competence. This point is often misunderstood, so it is worth spelling out in some detail. The argument is not a speculation about the feelings of persons who may or may not be the beneficiaries of affirmative action. Rather, it turns on the rational, statistical inferences that neutral observers are entitled to make about the unknown qualifications of persons who may have been preferred, or rejected, in a selection process.

The main insight is not difficult to grasp. Let some employer use a lower threshold of assessed productivity for the hiring of blacks than whites. The preferential hiring policy defines three categories of individuals within each of the two racial groups which I will call "marginals," "successes," and "failures." Marginals are those whose hiring status is altered by the policy—either whites not hired who otherwise would have been, or blacks hired who otherwise would not have been. Successes are those who would be hired with or without the policy, and failures are those who would be passed over with or without the preferential policy. Let us consider how an outsider who can observe the hiring decision, but not the employer's productivity assessment, would estimate the productivity of those subject to this hiring process.

Lower Hiring Thresholds

Notice that a lower hiring threshold for blacks causes the outside market to reduce its estimate of the productivity of black successes, since, on average, less is required to achieve that status. In addition, black failures, seen to have been passed over despite a lower hiring threshold, are thereby revealed as especially unproductive. On the other hand, a hiring process favoring blacks must enhance the reputations of white failures, as seen by outsiders, since they may have been artificially held back. And white successes, who are hired despite being disfavored in selection, have thereby been shown to be especially productive.

We have thus reached the result that, among blacks, only marginals gain from the establishment of a preferential hiring program—they do so because the outside observer lumps them together with black successes. They thus gain a job and a better reputation than they objectively deserve. Moreover, among whites, only marginals are harmed by the program, for only they lose the chance of securing a job and only they see their reputations harmed by virtue of being placed in the same category as white failures. In practical terms, since marginals are typically a minority of all workers, the outside reputations of most blacks will be lowered, and that of most whites enhanced, by preferential hiring. The inferential logic that leads to this arresting conclusion is particularly insidious, in that it can serve to legitimate otherwise indefensible negative stereotypes about blacks.

Patronization

Another reason for being skeptical about the practice of affirmative action is that it can undercut the incentives for blacks to develop their competitive abilities. For instance, preferential treatment can lead to the patronization of black workers and students. By "patronization," I mean the setting of lower standards of expected accomplishment for blacks than for whites because of the belief that blacks are not as capable of meeting a higher, common standard. In the 1993 article "Will Affirmative Action Eliminate Negative Stereotypes?" Stephen Coate and I show how behavior of this kind can be based on a self-fulfilling prophesy. That is, observed performance among blacks may be lower precisely because blacks are being patronized, a policy that is undertaken because of the need for an employer or admissions officer to meet affirmative-action guidelines.

Consider a workplace in which a supervisor operating under some affirmative-action guidelines must recommend subordinate workers for promotion. Suppose further that he is keen to promote blacks where possible, and that he monitors his subordinates' performance and bases his recommendations on these observations. Pressure to promote blacks might lead him to deemphasize deficiencies in the performance of black subordinates, recommending them for promotion when he would not have done so for whites. But his behavior could undermine the ability of black workers to identify and correct their deficiencies. They are denied honest feedback from their supervisor on their performance and are encouraged to think that one can get ahead without attaining the same degree of proficiency as whites. . . .

Affirmative Action as Common Sense

I am arguing that if our interest is achieving a just society, then there is nothing in the sorry history of affirmative action abuses that requires us to tie our hands with a color-blind formalism. Consider the common sense observation that, in this country, an army where blacks are one-third of the enlisted personnel but only three percent of the officer corps is likely to function poorly. The U.S. Army cares about the number of black captains because it needs to sustain effective cooperation among its personnel across racial lines. That the racial identities of captains and corporals sometimes matters to the smooth functioning of a military institution is a deep fact about our society, one that cannot be wished away. Now, monitoring the number of blacks promoted to the rank of captain, and formulating policies to increase that number, are activities that inherently involve taking account of some individual's race. Yet, depending on how they are undertaken, such activities need not entail the promulgation of racial double standards, nor need they seem to declare, as a matter of official policy, that racial identity is a determinant of an individual's moral worth. As the military sociologist Charles Moskos is fond of pointing out, the Army is the only place in American society where large numbers of whites routinely take orders from blacks. Ironically, the irrelevance of race to a person's moral worth may be more evident to the members of this institution than elsewhere in our society precisely because the government has taken account of race in the conduct of its military personnel policies.

Rejecting the Color-Blind Principle

The color-blind principle, while consistent as a self-contained legal rule, is in my opinion neither morally nor politically coherent. It requires that we not care about racial inequality, per se, when, as I have argued above, there are many compelling reasons to reject that position. For instance, the color-blind principle would seem to imply that we should discontinue all racial classifications associated with the collection of government statistics. To what proper use could the agencies possibly put the racial information—on crime, housing, employment, welfare receipt, test scores—which they collect? Yet, monitoring the racial dimension of social and economic trends is an obviously vital public function. Why? For one reason, consider that these data are the sole source of our knowledge that discrimination has declined over the years, a key aspect of the case for reforming the practice of affirmative action. Moreover, without these data, the vast overrepresentation of blacks among imprisoned felons in this country could not be rationalized in such a way as to refute the charge of systematic racism in the administration of criminal justice. These examples illustrate how, despite the moral irrelevance of race at the individual level, there remains an operational need to attend to racial disparity in the conduct of our public affairs.

Moreover, as I have suggested, racially targeted recruitment and racially defined anti-discrimination enforcement mechanisms inevitably entail a form of mild "reverse discrimination," because they guarantee a labor market environment in which the targeted group receives more favorable treatment. Color-blind employment policy, if faithfully and uniformly pursued, must mean the abolition of racial representation as a goal.

"A comparison of race-neutral and race-operative classifications reveals that race-neutral affirmative action is substantially less likely to reflect stereotypical, illegitimate motivations, or to have harmful effects."

Race-Neutral Affirmative Action Can Help the Disadvantaged

Kim Forde-Mazrui

Kim Forde-Mazrui is an associate law professor at the University of Virginia.

Reasoning that the Adarand *requirement of strict scrutiny may doom governmental affirmative action programs, Forde-Mazrui advises that race-neutral programs will remedy societal discrimination. Race-neutral affirmative action, she proposes, is less likely to stereotype, use illegitimate motivations or inflict harmful effects than race-based plans. A common example of a race-neutral plan classifies according to a tangible disadvantage, such as poverty; therefore, all members within the parameters of that disadvantaged group would receive the benefits of affirmative action. Since the results of race-neutral affirmative action plans are less likely to stir racial resentment and stereotyping, the programs, she believes, may reduce the significance of race.*

Kim Forde-Mazrui, "The Constitutional Implications of Race-Neutral Affirmative Action," *Georgetown Law Journal*, vol. 88, no. 8, August 2000, pp. 2331–98. Reproduced by permission.

In 1989, in *City of Richmond v. J.A. Croson Co.*, a consensus was finally reached by a majority of the Court that state-sponsored benign racial classifications are presumptively invalid and are subject to strict scrutiny. Although in the following year the Court held the federal government to a more lenient standard, it held in 1995, in *Adarand Constructors, Inc. v. Pena*, that federally enacted benign classifications are also subject to strict scrutiny. The principal significance of these decisions is the holding that benign racial classifications are as constitutionally troublesome or "suspect" as racial classifications that disadvantage racial minorities. By subjecting benign racial classifications to strict scrutiny, these decisions may have far-reaching implications for government-sponsored affirmative action. First, the nature of the strict scrutiny test articulated by the Court suggests that no affirmative action program employing a racial classification could withstand legal challenge. All such classifications thus may be doomed. Second, *Croson* and *Adarand* may spell the end to all government-sponsored efforts to remedy past discrimination or promote racial diversity, even when such efforts are pursued through race-neutral classifications. . . .

Race-Based Plans Fail Strict Scrutiny

The Court . . . has not held that remedying societal discrimination is itself an illegitimate purpose or that it cannot support remedial relief of any form. The Court has instead emphasized the insufficiency of this remedial purpose based upon the nature of the means it is employed to justify—a racial classification or other race-operative remedy. Herein lies the real difference between remedying identified and societal discrimination for constitutional purposes: the insufficiency of the latter interest to define and thereby limit the scope of a race-operative remedy. Identified discrimination enables a governmental entity to limit its reliance on race to the extent minimally necessary to remedy the effects so identified. Societal discrimination, in contrast, provides less guidance as to who suffers its effects, who is most responsible for them, and when, if ever, it has been remedied. It is, in the Court's view, too "amorphous" and, as such, "provides no guidance for a legislative body to determine the precise scope of the injury it seeks to remedy." Accordingly, remedying societal discrimination cannot justify racial classifications analyzed under strict scrutiny, not because such an interest is insufficiently important, but because it is too ill-defined to constrain the use of race-based remedies.

Benefits of Race-Neutral Plans

Remedying societal discrimination should, however, be accepted as sufficiently compelling to pursue through race-neutral means. The Court's concerns over racial classifications that underlie its rejection of societal discrimination as a sufficient justification largely disappear when race-neutral means are employed instead. A comparison of race-neutral and race-operative classifications reveals that race-neutral affirmative action is substantially less likely to reflect stereotypical, illegitimate motivations, or to have harmful effects. The discussion shall first compare the use of race-neutral means to racial classifications with respect to the risk of harmful effects, and then will compare the two types of means as they bear on the risk of illegitimate purposes.

Regarding effects, race-neutral affirmative action avoids inflicting the immediate injury caused by programs administered on the basis of racial classifications. It is also less likely to exacerbate those race-related social problems identified by the Court, such as the perpetuation of stereotypes, inflaming racial hostility and, in general, delaying the day that race no longer has significance in American life. First, in terms of their immediate effect, the means used by race-neutral affirmative action, such as disadvantage-based classifications, are unobjectionable in the way they are administered. While racial classifications require those charged with their administration to identify and treat individuals differently on the basis of their race, and in so doing inflict "an injury that falls squarely within the language and spirit of the Constitution's guarantee of equal protection," race-neutral classifications can be executed without racial discrimination.

Stereotyping Avoided

Nor are race-neutral programs that classify on the basis of disadvantage likely to perpetuate the kind of stereotypical thinking with which the Court seems so concerned. Recall how racial classifications, by awarding benefits and burdens along racial lines, reinforce beliefs in the inferiority of racial minorities, who are treated as disadvantaged because of their race, and in the superiority of whites, who are treated as too privileged to deserve a compensatory preference. By contrast, race-neutral classifications based on disadvantage send a meaningfully different message. By their terms and operation, they award a preference to individuals who have been identified as suffering from a tangible disadvantage and deny such a preference to those not suffering from that disadvantage, and they do so on a basis open to all regardless of race. Such programs send the realistic message that people who suffer from material or other tangible disadvantages are, indeed, disadvantaged.

To the extent that race-neutral classifications have a racial message, it is that blacks and whites who suffer from similar disadvantages share a common condition, while whites and blacks who do not suffer such disadvantages share a relative privilege. Race is not, by the terms of the classification, a common denominator. Rather, the classification finds commonalities between members of different (and the same) races and finds differences between persons of the same (and different) races. The classification, in other words, by its very silence on race, sends the message that "race does not matter," a normative proposition that the Court and opponents of racial preferences purport to embrace.

Resentment Avoided

Race-neutral classifications are also less likely than race-operative classifications to cause racial divisiveness or resentment. As discussed earlier, much of the resentment over race-operative affirmative action stems from the way in which this kind of action both appears to give preferential treatment to some privileged racial minorities who do not deserve it and denies opportunities to disadvantaged white persons in need of help. Race-neutral affirmative action resolves both of these objections. Blacks who do not suffer from the identified disadvantage receive no benefit, and whites who do so suffer are benefited. The winners are disadvantaged blacks and whites, and the losers are advantaged blacks and whites. Such "losers" are unlikely to complain too loudly that those with less are being helped. Any resentment is at least unlikely to be as deeply held and racially defined as that fostered by racial preferences.

Remedial Benefits

The salutary [remedial] effects of race-neutral affirmative action can be seen in three other respects as well. First, a substantial number of white people would benefit from race-neutral, disadvantaged-based programs, likely reducing the risk of white resentment engendered by minority-exclusive preferences. Among the poor, although a disproportionate share are racial minorities as compared to the percentage of whites so disadvantaged, there are at least as many whites as minorities in actual numbers. A program designed to benefit the poor, therefore, would benefit as many whites as minorities. When one moves up the economic ladder to the lower middle class, a substantial majority of this class is white. That is why, especially in the context of higher education, the majority of those benefited by disadvantage-based programs are likely to be white. While the ineffectiveness of such an approach in creating racial diversity has led some to criticize race-neutral affirmative action, the fact that the beneficiaries of such efforts will include so many whites should soften concerns that the interests of whites were unfairly ignored in designing the program. The ineffectiveness of race-neutral classifications at benefiting only or mainly racial minorities may thus be a virtue from a constitutional standpoint.

Targets Actual Victims

Indeed, if one considers only the beneficiaries outside the target group of actual victims of discrimination, race-neutral affirmative action probably does not benefit minorities even in proportional terms, and not just in actual numbers. Since affirmative action is problematic only to the extent it fails to benefit or "fit" only true victims of discrimination, it seems legitimate to inquire how nonvictims of discrimination are actually affected. If we assume that, absent discrimination, the races would be represented in rough ... proportion among the disadvantaged, then disadvantage-based programs disproportionately benefit racial minorities because of discrimination. It follows that the disproportionate number of minorities compared to whites that benefit from disadvantage-based programs roughly represents the number of actual victims of discrimination. The remaining disadvantaged persons that benefit from disadvantage-based programs—those who are not disadvantaged because of discrimination—should include a roughly proportional percentage of different races, including whites. Accordingly, among the "undeserving" beneficiaries of a race-neutral disadvantage-based program, a proportional share is white. Thus, to the extent that race-neutral affirmative action "misses" discrimination victims, and instead benefits people who are not disadvantaged from discrimination, it does not favor racial minorities after all.

Plan Duration Irrelevant

Second, as compared with racial preferences, there is little reason to be concerned about the length of time a race-neutral program remains in effect. Racial preferences that cause discrimination against whites are, at best, regrettable and few observers would want to see them continue indefinitely. Moreover, as racial preferences succeed in their purpose, they become more unfair in a racial sense. That is, as racial minorities become less disadvantaged compared to whites, fewer minorities who benefit from racial preferences will truly need or deserve it. Recall that these concerns seem to underlie the Court's rejection of societal discrimination as a justification for racial preferences because it "provides no logical stopping point." The need to make race-neutral affirmative action temporary, by contrast, is less obvious. Not only do such programs avoid racially discriminatory treatment in their administration, but also as they succeed in remedying the effects of societal discrimination, their racially disparate impact should decline. That is, if race-neutral affirmative action succeeds in reducing racial disparities, then the (arguably) disparate impact of such programs in favor of racial minorities will be reduced. While initially conceived as an effort to remedy racial discrimination, race-neutral affirmative action programs could be retained indefinitely as legitimate programs that help disadvantaged persons without regard to race.

Plan All-Inclusive

Third, race-neutral classifications avoid the necessity of choosing which racial groups to include in a preferential program, which groups not to include, and how to define such groups. With racial classifications, a choice of which racial groups to prefer is required, a choice that may appear arbitrary or unjustified for some groups compared to others that may have experienced more severe discrimination. Indeed, even the process of defining racial groups and deciding which are more "deserving" than others has a certain unseemliness. Moreover, such potentially offensive racial sorting might have to be repeated on a regular basis as changes occur in the relative status of different racial groups. Race-neutral classifications, by contrast, largely avoid these pitfalls. Because people receive benefits on the basis of disadvantage, anyone so disadvantaged is eligible, regardless of race, avoiding the need to choose, define, or categorize people by race. To the extent that different racial groups have suffered discrimination or are otherwise disadvantaged to different degrees, disadvantage-based preferences provide a sort of "rough justice" without racial sorting. Nor would re-sorting be required because, first, racial sorting is not involved at the outset and, second, any changes in the relative positions of racial groups would be automatically captured by the disadvantage-based preference. If some groups were to become more or less privileged compared to others, they would benefit proportionately less or more by need-based programs.

Future Benefit

The effects of race-neutral affirmative action, both immediately and consequentially, are thus substantially less objectionable than racial classifications with respect to the Court's concerns. Race-neutral classifications are significantly less likely than racial classifications to perpetuate racial stereotypes or racial hostility and, by their very terms, encourage the transformation of race-based thinking to an approach based on more tangible race-neutral conditions shared or not shared by people regardless of race. Thus, to the extent the Court seems to have placed constitutional significance on the effects affirmative action may have in perpetuating and exacerbating race-conscious attitudes, race-neutral remedial programs are significantly less likely to foster—and may instead help to diminish—the relevance of race.

Illegitimate Motivations

Next, consider the risk of illegitimate motivations with which strict scrutiny is also concerned. Here, too, race-neutral classifications are substantially less troublesome than race-based classifications. By classifying on the basis of tangible disadvantage and not race, race-neutral remedial policies are less likely than racial classifications to stem from illegitimate racial purposes or beliefs. Recall that one function of strict scrutiny is to "smoke out" illegitimate purposes by constraining the legislature to means that only serve compelling interests, thereby leaving little room for active pursuit of impermissible goals. The risk is significant that illegitimate purposes, such as prejudice, stereotypes, and simple racial politics, motivated racial classifications because such classifications plausibly serve these purposes. That is, many of the immediate and consequential effects caused by racial classifications, effects that make such classifications objectionable in themselves, contribute to the inference that illegitimate purposes may have motivated them. A classification that embodies, and thereby perpetuates, the stereotype that racial minorities are inherently disadvantaged and deserving of race-based preferential treatment serves the purpose of a legislature that believes this to be true. A racial classification that benefits racial minorities, regardless of whether individuals within the benefited class are truly disadvantaged, and which ignores or burdens the opportunities of whites who suffer from disadvantage, serves the purpose of a legislature captured by simple racial politics in which political power is exercised for the sake of racial minorities alone. A law that racially classifies, and thereby treats people differently on the basis of race, serves the purpose of a legislature that believes race to be a relevant and important character trait, in violation of the normative position of the Court that race is rarely relevant.

A Legitimate Remedy

In contrast, a race-neutral law that operates directly on the basis of disadvantage in by its own terms a close "fit" to the purpose of helping those truly disadvantaged, some of whom are disadvantaged because of societal discrimination and others for other reasons. A remedial program that helps blacks and whites identically with respect to similarly shared race-neutral disadvantages, and which fails to help blacks and whites who share similar advantages, serves the purpose of a legislature dedicated to moving from a mode of categorizing persons on the basis of race to one that views any differences among people to be based on tangible conditions and experiences, not skin color.

"Mandatory court-ordered affirmative action would present a controversial addition to civil rights law."

Mandatory Affirmative Action Is Needed in the Workplace

Kenneth R. Davis

Kenneth R. Davis is an associate professor of legal and ethical studies at Fordham University Graduate School of Business Administration.

In the following selection, Davis addresses the impassioned debate over whether affirmative action achieves social justice or ratifies reverse discrimination. The author indicates that court-ordered affirmative action would deter employers from racial discrimination, yet some criticize it as oppressive for those employers that discriminate unintentionally.

D enounced by some and praised by others, affirmative action inflames emotions and incites debate. Critics label affirmative action a euphemism, a twist of linguistic chicanery that condones reverse discrimination. Supporters hail it as an enlightened imperative for achieving social justice. . . .

Affirmative Action Is Predominantly Voluntary

An approach to break the stranglehold of racial discrimination, affirmative action takes a person's race into account in making decisions, particularly in the areas of employment and

Kenneth R. Davis. "Undo Hardship: An Argument for Affirmative Action as a Mandatory Remedy in Systemic Racial Discrimination Cases," *Dickinson Law Review*, vol. 107, no. 3, winter 2003, pp. 503–70. Reproduced by permission.

education. Affirmative action is predominantly voluntary. Its success in the workplace depends on the good will of employers who choose to consider race in hiring and promotion decisions. Even freedom to do good deeds has its limits. Because affirmative action plans sometimes unfairly penalize unprotected workers, voluntary affirmative action plans must conform to the legal requirements of Title VII of the 1964 Civil Rights Act (Title VII). To prevent voluntary affirmative action programs from deteriorating into platforms for reverse discrimination, the Supreme Court, in *United Steelworkers of America v. Weber* and *Johnson v. Transportation Agency*, held that affirmative action plans must apply only to job categories in which minorities are traditionally underrepresented. Such plans may not exalt race over merit as a job qualification.

The duty to make reasonable accommodations for employees is legally distinct from affirmative action, but the two concepts are interwoven. This duty finds limited application under Title VII, for while a diluted version of reasonable accommodation applies to religious discrimination cases, it does not apply at all to cases of discrimination based on race, sex, or national origin. The duty to provide reasonable accommodations, however, is indispensable in disability cases. Most notably, Title I of the Americans with Disabilities Act (ADA) requires employers make reasonable accommodations for individuals with disabilities who can perform essential job functions when such accommodations are in place.

In passing the ADA and creating the employer's duty to make reasonable accommodations, Congress recognized that disabled people "occupy an inferior status" in society. Disability civil rights law, including the duty to provide reasonable accommodations, seeks to abolish this caste system. Another rationale for applying the reasonable accommodation principle to disability cases is that some disabled individuals can be productive workers if employers take measures to diminish the effects of disabilities on workplace performance. When a reasonable accommodation removes the hampering effect of a disability, the worker, the employer, and society benefit.

Comparing Race and Disabilities

One may analogize disability cases to race cases. Physical and mental impairments and unfounded stereotypes hinder the disabled from getting jobs. Similarly, an impoverished environment, racial stereotypes, and a contracted range of educational and employment opportunities constrain minority workers, particularly African-Americans, from achieving in all phases of their lives, including on the job. These disadvantages, which might be called "societally induced racial disabilities," hinder African-Americans in the same way that physical and mental disabilities hinder the disabled. Members of both classes—African-Americans and the disabled—are able to perform essential job functions with "reasonable accommodations." In the context of racial discrimination, a reasonable accommodation might take the form of a traditional affirmative action plan aimed at increasing the number of blacks in an employer's workforce, or affirmative action might take the form of a special recruiting and training program aimed to overcome the educational or experiential disadvantages of identified minority workers.

Although reasonable accommodation and affirmative action are not identical, reasonable accommodation is comparable to affirmative action in according a preference to the protected class. Both concepts assume that the beneficiaries will perform essential job functions adequately. Both concepts entail costs to the employer, including direct and indirect expenses resulting from inefficiencies in the workplace. The purpose of both concepts is to eradicate stereotypes, stigmas, and the effects of disadvantage, whether physical, mental, or social. The scope of the preference that reasonable accommodation affords the disabled often equals and sometimes exceeds the scope of the preference that affirmative action affords minorities.

Affirmative Action Is Not Mandatory for Blacks

Despite the bias against African-Americans that persists in our society, Congress has not created an analogous duty to accommodate blacks in the workplace by making some form of affirmative action mandatory. Many reasons account for Congress's inaction. First, many in Congress oppose affirmative action on moral and practical grounds. Second, Congress must respond to popular sentiment, much of which objects to race-conscious affirmative action. Many may be more responsive to the needs of the disabled rather than the needs of minorities, because physical disabilities are more visible than societally induced disadvantages. Third, race is a constitutionally suspect classification, whereas disability is not. Thus, any race-conscious classification must meet the most rigorous constitutional test.

Private Employers

Of course, Congress would never create a general duty for all private employers to adopt affirmative action plans, and, if it did, outrage would thunder throughout the nation. Aside from being politically untenable, such a law would violate the guarantee of equal protection under the Fifth and Fourteenth Amendments. There is, however, a more limited and less provocative means of mandating affirmative action. The approach is court-ordered affirmative action. Section 706(g) of Title VII provides that a court may "order such affirmative action as may be appropriate," as a remedy for civil rights violations. Because court orders are state action, court-ordered affirmative action plans must meet not only the requirements of Title VII but also those of the Equal Protection Clause of the Fourteenth Amendment or the equal protection component of the Due Process Clause of the Fifth Amendment. Unlike a global duty to engage in affirmative action, appropriate court-ordered affirmative action does not offend the Constitution because courts impose the duty to engage in affirmative action against only those who have violated civil rights law.

Egregious or Persistent Violations

The Supreme Court has provided guidance as to the constitutional standard applicable to affirmative action remedies. In *Local 28 of Sheet Metal Workers International Association v. EEOC*, the Supreme Court suggested that the Constitution confines such relief to egregious or persistent violations. The Court's suggestion was wrong. All statistical civil rights violations are serious enough to justify appropriately tailored affirmative action. No civil rights violation is ordinary. The Court seemed to recognize this in the *Sheet Metal Workers* decision by stating that the Constitution permits court-ordered affirmative action to eliminate "the lingering effects of pervasive discrimination," a requirement that arguably applies to any systemic civil rights violation.

The primacy of the policy to eradicate racial discrimination supports mandatory court-ordered affirmative action in systemic racial discrimination cases. Making affirmative action mandatory, where statistical violations are proven, would place the policy to rid the workplace of racial discrimination on an equal footing with the policy to rid the workplace of discrimination against the disabled. This article proposes that the applicable constitutional standard, the strict scrutiny test, is met even when statistical violations fall short of "egregious or persistent." Strict scrutiny is satisfied when the defendant violates Title VII either by engaging in a pattern and practice of discrimination or by engaging in disparate impact discrimination. Both violations are based on a significant disparity between the workforce of the employer and the relevant labor market. Affirmative action is the most effective measure to end the effects of such violations. . . .

The Continuing Controversy

The controversy over what remedies should be available to disadvantaged minorities seems never to abate. The argument is a nagging splinter in the body politic. Issues debated in 1964 occupy scholars today. Opinions voiced on television news programs echo concerns raised in Congress forty years ago. Some advocate more drastic approaches such as the payment of reparations, while others complain that even voluntary affirmative action goes too far.

Affirmative action is akin to reasonable accommodation. They may not be identical twins, but they are hard to tell apart. Both remedies seek to rid the disadvantaged of the debilitating effects of obstacles to employment. The symptoms hindering the physically and mentally disabled are more palpable than those that hinder racial minorities, but the effects are the same. An education that ended after the seventh grade is a burden. Life in an impoverished environment is another burden. Immersion in a society that tells you on television, in magazines, on the street, and in the workplace that you are not as worthy as white people is perhaps the greatest burden of all. Societally induced racial disability deserves the same legal recognition as physical and mental disabilities. The stereotype of racial inferiority is as harmful as the belief that the disabled are incapable of putting in a good day's work.

Mandatory Affirmative Action Would Provide Consistency

If affirmative action is viewed as a reasonable accommodation, it should, for the sake of consistency in the law, be mandatory in appropriate cases. The issue becomes how to fashion the mandatory remedy consistent with constitutional principles. *Sheet Metal Workers* and *Paradise* have blessed court-ordered affirmative action, but *Croson* and *Adarand* require that court-ordered affirmative action meet the strict scrutiny test. The government has a compelling state interest in eradicating discrimination. This compelling state interest justifies mandatory court-ordered affirmative action in appropriate cases. Disparate impact and pattern and practice cases are ripe for mandatory court-ordered affirmative action because both types of violations involve statistical disparities between the employer's workforce and the relevant labor market. Affirmative action is an indispensable method for rectifying such disparities. As long as the plan is narrowly tailored, mandatory court-ordered affirmative action in such cases satisfies strict scrutiny.

To ensure fairness and efficacy, affirmative action plans should be subject to continuing judicial supervision. The district court presiding over the case should have the authority, at the remedy stage, to order the defendant or a court-appointed administrator to submit a mandatory affirmative action plan for judicial consideration. The plan could propose any of a number of strategies including race-conscious hiring and training practices and special educational, supervisory, and apprenticeship programs for minorities. Before approving the plan, the court should consider the plan's feasibility and probability of success, giving due consideration to the company's financial condition and its other resources.

Mandatory Affirmative Action Is Controversial

Mandatory court-ordered affirmative action would present a controversial addition to civil rights law. Some would argue that the proposal would oppress employers responsible merely for unintentional violations of Title VII. It is true that mandatory court-ordered affirmative action, as proposed in this article, would raise the stakes for offenders. But, in doing so, it might deter violations. Although disparate impact is by definition unintentional, employers faced with the prospect of mandatory affirmative action would likely sift through their employment practices to rid themselves of those that might instigate an unhappy judicial encounter. Critics will object that the proposal would erect obstacles blocking non-minority workers from employment opportunities. One might better focus, however, on the other side of the argument: The proposal would foster equality of opportunity for the population of African-Americans, and achieving such equality is at the heart of civil rights law.

CHAPTER 4

College Admissions

Case Overview

Grutter v. Bollinger (2003)

Ever since the mixed messages of the landmark decision *Regents of the University of California v. Bakke* in 1978, colleges and universities have sought to fashion affirmative-action plans to increase diversity on their campuses. The majority opinion by Justice Lewis Powell in the *Bakke* case struck down the use of quotas, yet upheld diversity as a compelling goal.

The Powell opinion laid the groundwork for *Grutter v. Bollinger*, a challenge to the University of Michigan Law School's admission program. In the majority decision, Justice Sandra Day O'Connor addressed the claim of Barbara Grutter, a white Michigan resident, who claimed that the law school discriminated against her by denying her admission. Grutter alleged that the admission program used race as a "predominant" factor in its decision to reject her application, and thus violated the Equal Protection Clause of the Fourteenth Amendment. Additionally, she argued that the law school lacked a compelling state interest in using race as a factor, especially if it harmed another race.

Relying heavily on the standards mandated by Justice Powell in *Bakke*, the majority opinion in *Grutter* held that the law school's narrowly tailored use of race in admission decisions promoted a compelling interest in obtaining the educational benefits that flow from a diverse student body; therefore, the use of race is not prohibited by the Constitution, specifically the Equal Protection Clause of the Fourteenth Amendment, nor does the admission policy violate Title VI of the Civil Rights Act of 1964.

Justice O'Connor emphasized that the Court must carefully consider the context when reviewing race-based actions. Even though all government racial preferences must be analyzed by a reviewing court under strict scrutiny, not all racial preferences are invalidated by this high degree of examination. Rather, strict scrutiny determines whether a racially preferential plan is benign and necessary. In *Grutter*, the Court deferred to the law school's judgment that diversity is necessary to the pursuit of its educational mission. Justice O'Connor agreed that diversity enhances cross-racial understanding and breaks down racial stereotypes. Expert studies indicate that diversity promotes learning outcomes and better prepares students for the legal profession, as well as a multicultural workforce and society. Universities, especially law schools, represent a training ground for a substantial number of the country's leaders. Therefore, the Court reasoned, diversity is a compelling interest

The law school's admission plan was interpreted as being narrowly tailored since it is flexible enough to consider each applicant as an individual. Correspondingly, race may be considered as a "plus" factor in a particular student's file. Previous court decisions have made clear that colleges may not use quotas or put members of a disadvantaged group on a separate admission track. The University of Michigan Law School's admission plan is both individualistic and holistic in that an applicant's review considers all factors, not just G.P.A. and the LSAT (Law School Admission Test). As such, it does not unduly harm students of the traditionally favored race. In reference to the requirement that any plan using racial preferences must be limited in duration, the law school maintained that it looks forward to the time when a race-neutral formula will replace a race-based program. The majority opinion expressed the hope that in twenty-five years, the use of racial classifications will be unnecessary.

The *Grutter* decision is important in several ways. First, it proved that an affirmative-action plan can survive strict scrutiny. Second, it reiterated that diversity represents a valid goal and that higher education constitutes a special category in affirmative-action analysis. Finally, the Court's decision offered the law school's admission program as an example of an affirmative-action plan that does not violate the Constitution. Racial preferences, therefore, may be permitted as long as race is one of many considerations and not the predominant factor.

> "[T]he diffusion of knowledge and op-
> portunity through public institutions of
> higher education must be accessible to
> all individuals regardless of race or eth-
> nicity."

The Court's Decision: Racial Preferences Are Permitted to Achieve Student Diversity

Sandra Day O'Connor

Sandra Day O'Connor, the first woman on the Supreme Court, was appointed to the Court in 1981. A centrist, she served on the Court until her retirement in 2006.

Justice O'Connor, in her majority opinion, states that although all government racial classifications must be analyzed by a court under strict scrutiny, not all race-based action is invalid. If a racial classification is deemed necessary to further a compelling governmental interest, the Equal Protection Clause is not violated as long as the classification is narrowly tailored. Justice O'Connor concludes that student body diversity, which promotes learning and interracial understanding, is a compelling state interest that justifies using race in university admissions. The University of Michigan Law School admission program is flexible and gives applicants individual attention without the use of quotas, which are prohibited. Since race-based plans must be limited in duration, as the law school concedes, the Court hopes that in twenty-five years the use of racial preferences will no longer be needed.

Sandra Day O'Connor, majority opinion, *Grutter v. Bollinger*, 539 U.S. 306, 2003.

The [University of Michigan Law School] ranks among the Nation's top law schools. It receives more than 3,500 applications each year for a class of around 350 students. Seeking to "admit a group of students who individually and collectively are among the most capable," the Law School looks for individuals with "substantial promise for success in law school" and "a strong likelihood of succeeding in the practice of law and contributing in diverse ways to the well-being of others." More broadly, the Law School seeks "a mix of students with varying backgrounds and experiences who will respect and learn from each other." In 1992, the dean of the Law School charged a faculty committee with crafting a written admissions policy to implement these goals. In particular, the Law School sought to ensure that its efforts to achieve student body diversity complied with this Court's most recent ruling on the use of race in university admissions. See *Regents of Univ. of Cal. v. Bakke* (1978). Upon the unanimous adoption of the committee's report by the Law School faculty, it became the Law School's official admissions policy.

The hallmark of that policy is its focus on academic ability coupled with a flexible assessment of applicants' talents, experiences, and potential "to contribute to the learning of those around them." The policy requires admissions officials to evaluate each applicant based on all the information available in the file, including a personal statement, letters of recommendation, and an essay describing the ways in which the applicant will contribute to the life and diversity of the Law School. In reviewing an applicant's file, admissions officials must consider the applicant's undergraduate grade point average (GPA) and Law School Admissions Test (LSAT) score because they are important (if imperfect) predictors of academic success in law school. The policy stresses that "no applicant should be admitted unless we expect that applicant to do well enough to graduate with no serious academic problems." . . .

Petitioner Barbara Grutter is a white Michigan resident who applied to the Law School in 1996 with a 3.8 grade point average and 161 LSAT score. The Law School initially placed petitioner on a waiting list, but subsequently rejected her application. . . .

Petitioner further alleged that her application was rejected because the Law School uses race as a "predominant" factor, giving applicants who belong to certain minority groups "a significantly greater chance of admission than students with similar credentials from disfavored racial groups." . . .

Justice Powell's Diversity Rationale

We last addressed the use of race in public higher education over 25 years ago. In the landmark *Bakke* case, we reviewed a racial set-aside program that reserved 16 out of 100 seats in a medical school class for members of certain minority groups. The decision produced six separate opinions, none of which commanded a majority of the Court. Four Justices would have upheld the program against all attack on the ground that the government can use race to "remedy disadvantages cast on minorities by past racial prejudice." Four other Justices avoided the constitutional question altogether and struck down the program on statutory grounds. Justice Powell provided a fifth vote not only for invalidating the set-aside program, but also for reversing the state court's injunction against any use of race whatsoever. The only holding for the Court in *Bakke* was that a "State has a substantial interest that legitimately may be served by a properly devised admissions program involving the competitive consideration of race and ethnic origin." Thus, we reversed that part of the lower court's judgment that enjoined the university "from any consideration of the race of any applicant."

Since this Court's splintered decision in *Bakke*, Justice Powell's opinion announcing the judgment of the Court has served as the touchstone for constitutional analysis of race-conscious admissions policies. Public and private universities across the Nation have modeled their own admissions programs on Justice Powell's views on permissible race-conscious policies.

Justice Powell began by stating that "[t]he guarantee of equal protection cannot mean one thing when applied to one individual and something else when applied to a person of another color. If both are not accorded the same protection, then it is not equal." In Justice Powell's view, when governmental decisions "touch upon an individual's race or ethnic background, he is entitled to a judicial determination that the burden he is asked to bear on that basis is precisely tailored to serve a compelling governmental interest." . . .

The Importance of Strict Scrutiny

The Equal Protection Clause provides that no State shall "deny to any person within its jurisdiction the equal protection of the laws." U.S. Const. Amendment 14, §2. Because the Fourteenth Amendment "protect[s] *persons*, not *groups*," all "governmental action based on race—a *group* classification long recognized as in most circumstances irrelevant and therefore prohibited—should be subjected to detailed judicial inquiry to ensure that the *personal* right to equal protection of the laws has not been infringed" [*Adarand Constructors, Inc. v. Peña* (1995)]. We are a free people whose institutions are founded upon the doctrine of equality. It follows from that principle that "government may treat people differently because of their race only for the most compelling reasons."

We have held that all racial classifications imposed by government must be analyzed by a reviewing court under strict scrutiny. This means that such classifications are constitutional only if they are narrowly tailored to further compelling governmental interests. Absent searching judicial inquiry into the justification for such race-based measures, we have no way to determine what classifications are benign or remedial and what classifications are in fact motivated by illegitimate notions of racial inferiority or simple racial politics. We apply strict scrutiny to all racial classifications to smoke out illegitimate uses of race by assuring that [government] is pursuing a goal important enough to warrant use of a highly suspect tool.

Strict scrutiny is not strict in theory, but fatal in fact. Although all governmental uses of race are subject to strict scrutiny, not all are invalidated by it. As we have explained, whenever the government treats any person unequally because of his or her race, that person has suffered an injury that falls squarely within the language and spirit of the Constitution's guarantee of equal protection. But that observation says nothing about the ultimate validity of any particular law; that determination is the job of the court applying strict scrutiny. When race-based action is necessary to further a compelling governmental interest, such action does not violate the constitutional guarantee of equal protection so long as the narrow-tailoring requirement is also satisfied.

Context matters when reviewing race-based governmental action under the Equal Protection Clause. In *Adarand Constructors, Inc. v. Peña*, we made clear that strict scrutiny must take "'relevant differences' into account." ... Not every decision influenced by race is equally objectionable and strict scrutiny is designed to provide a framework for carefully examining the importance and the sincerity of the reasons advanced by the governmental decisionmaker for the use of race in that particular context.

Deference to University's Diversity Goal

With these principles in mind, we turn to the question whether the Law School's use of race is justified by a compelling state interest. Before this Court, as they have throughout this litigation, respondents assert only one justification for their use of race in the admissions process: obtaining "the educational benefits that flow from a diverse student body." In other words, the Law School asks us to recognize, in the context of higher education, a compelling state interest in student body diversity.

We first wish to dispel the notion that the Law School's argument has been foreclosed, either expressly or implicitly, by our affirmative-action cases decided since *Bakke*. It is true that some language in those opinions might be read to suggest that remedying past discrimination is the only permissible justification for race-based governmental action. But we have never held that the only governmental use of race that can survive strict scrutiny is remedying past discrimination. Nor, since *Bakke*, have we directly addressed the use of race in the context of public higher education. Today, we hold that the Law School has a compelling interest in attaining a diverse student body.

The Law School's educational judgment that such diversity is essential to its educational mission is one to which we defer. The Law School's assessment that diversity will, in fact, yield educational benefits is substantiated by respondents and their *amici* [*amici curiae* refers to briefs submitted by interested parties]. Our scrutiny of the interest asserted by the Law School is no less strict for taking into account complex educational judgments in an area that lies primarily within the expertise of the university. Our holding today is in keeping with our tradition of giving a degree of deference to a university's academic decisions, within constitutionally prescribed limits.

We have long recognized that, given the important purpose of public education and the expansive freedom of speech and thought associated with the university environment, universities occupy a special niche in our constitutional tradition. . . .

Our conclusion that the Law School has a compelling interest in a diverse student body is informed by our view that attaining a diverse student body is at the heart of the Law

School's proper institutional mission, and that good faith on the part of a university is presumed absent a showing to the contrary.

Benefits of Diversity

As part of its goal of assembling a class that is both exceptionally academically qualified and broadly diverse, the Law School seeks to enroll a "critical mass" of minority students. The Law School's interest is not simply "to assure within its student body some specified percentage of a particular group merely because of its race or ethnic origin." That would amount to outright racial balancing, which is patently unconstitutional. Rather, the Law School's concept of critical mass is defined by reference to the educational benefits that diversity is designed to produce.

These benefits are substantial. As the District Court emphasized, the Law School's admissions policy promotes "cross-racial understanding," helps to break down racial stereotypes, and "enables [students] to better understand persons of different races." These benefits are "important and laudable," because "classroom discussion is livelier, more spirited, and simply more enlightening and interesting" when the students have "the greatest possible variety of backgrounds."

The Law School's claim of a compelling interest is further bolstered by its *amici*, who point to the educational benefits that flow from student body diversity. In addition to the expert studies and reports entered into evidence at trial, numerous studies show that student body diversity promotes learning outcomes, and better prepares students for an increasingly diverse workforce and society, and better prepares them as professionals. . . .

We have repeatedly acknowledged the overriding importance of preparing students for work and citizenship, describing education as pivotal to sustaining our political and cultural heritage with a fundamental role in maintaining the fabric of society. For this reason, the diffusion of knowledge and opportunity through public institutions of higher education must be accessible to all individuals regardless of race or ethnicity. The United States, as *amicus curiae*, affirms that "[e]nsuring that public institutions are open and available to all segments of American society, including people of all races and ethnicities, represents a paramount government objective." . . . Effective participation by members of all racial and ethnic groups in the civic life of our Nation is essential if the dream of one Nation, indivisible, is to be realized.

Moreover, universities, and in particular, law schools, represent the training ground for a large number of our Nation's leaders. Individuals with law degrees occupy roughly half the state governorships, more than half the seats in the United States Senate, and more than a third of the seats in the United States House of Representatives. . . .

University Plan Narrowly Tailored

Even in the limited circumstance when drawing racial distinctions is permissible to further a compelling state interest, government is still constrained in how it may pursue that end: [T]he means chosen to accomplish the [government's] asserted purpose must be specifically and narrowly framed to accomplish that purpose. The purpose of the narrow tailoring requirement is to ensure that "the means chosen 'fit' . . . th[e] compelling goal so closely that there is little or no possibility that the motive for the classification was illegitimate racial prejudice or stereotype."

Since *Bakke*, we have had no occasion to define the contours of the narrow-tailoring inquiry with respect to race-conscious university admissions programs. That inquiry must be calibrated to fit the distinct issues raised by the use of race to achieve student body diversity in public higher education. . . .

To be narrowly tailored, a race-conscious admissions program cannot use a quota system—it cannot insulat[e] each category of applicants with certain desired qualifications from competition with all other applicants. Instead, a university may consider race or ethnicity only as a "plus" in a particular applicant's file, without insulat[ing] the individual from comparison with all other candidates for the available seats. In other words, an admissions program must be flexible enough to consider all pertinent elements of diversity in light of the particular qualifications of each applicant, and to place them on the same footing for consideration, although not necessarily according them the same weight.

We find that the Law School's admissions program bears the hallmarks of a narrowly tailored plan. As Justice Powell made clear in *Bakke*, truly individualized consideration demands that race be used in a flexible, nonmechanical way. It follows from this mandate that universities cannot establish quotas for members of certain racial groups or put members of those groups on separate admissions tracks. Nor can universities insulate applicants who belong to certain racial or ethnic groups from the competition for admission. Universities can, however, consider race or ethnicity more flexibly as a "plus" factor in the context of individualized consideration of each and every applicant.

Quotas Not Allowed

We are satisfied that the Law School's admissions program, like the Harvard plan described by Justice Powell, does not operate as a quota. Properly understood, a "quota" is a program in which a certain fixed number or proportion of opportunities are reserved exclusively for certain minority groups. Quotas impose a fixed number or percentage which must be attained, or which cannot be exceeded, and insulate the individual from comparison with all other candidates for the available seats. In contrast, a permissible goal . . . require[s] only a good-faith effort ... to come within a range demarcated by the goal itself, and permits consideration of race as a "plus" factor in any given case while still ensuring that each candidate compete[s] with all other qualified applicants. . . .

The Law School's goal of attaining a critical mass of underrepresented minority students does not transform its program into a quota. As the Harvard plan described by Justice Powell recognized, there is of course "some relationship between numbers and achieving the benefits to be derived from a diverse student body, and between numbers and providing a reasonable environment for those students admitted." [S]ome attention to numbers, without more, does not transform a flexible admissions system into a rigid quota. . . .

That a race-conscious admissions program does not operate as a quota does not, by itself, satisfy the requirement of individualized consideration. When using race as a "plus" factor in university admissions, a university's admissions program must remain flexible enough to ensure that each applicant is evaluated as an individual and not in a way that makes an applicant's race or ethnicity the defining feature of his or her application. The importance of this individualized consideration in the context of a race-conscious admissions program is paramount.

Individual Review

Here, the Law School engages in a highly individualized, holistic review of each applicant's file, giving serious consideration to all the ways an applicant might contribute to a diverse educational environment. The Law School affords this individualized consideration to applicants of all races. There is no policy, either *de jure* [according to law] or *de facto* [accepted as law], of automatic acceptance or rejection based on any single "soft" variable. Unlike the program at issue in *Gratz v. Bollinger*, the Law School awards no mechanical, predetermined diversity "bonuses" based on race or ethnicity. Like the Harvard plan, the Law School's admissions policy is flexible enough to consider all pertinent elements of diversity in light of the particular qualifications of each applicant, and to place them on the same footing for consideration, although not necessarily according them the same weight.

We also find that, like the Harvard plan Justice Powell referenced in *Bakke*, the Law School's race-conscious admissions program adequately ensures that all factors that may contribute to student body diversity are meaningfully considered alongside race in admissions decisions. With respect to the use of race itself, all underrepresented minority students admitted by the Law School have been deemed qualified. By virtue of our Nation's struggle with racial inequality, such students are both likely to have experiences of particular importance to the Law School's mission, and less likely to be admitted in meaningful numbers on criteria that ignore those experiences. . . .

Race-Neutral Alternatives

Petitioner and the United States argue that the Law School's plan is not narrowly tailored because race-neutral means exist to obtain the educational benefits of student body diversity that the Law School seeks. We disagree. Narrow tailoring does not require exhaustion of every conceivable race-neutral alternative. Nor does it require a university to choose between maintaining a reputation for excellence or fulfilling a commitment to provide educational opportunities to members of all racial groups. Narrow tailoring does, however, require serious, good faith consideration of workable race-neutral alternatives that will achieve the diversity the university seeks.

We agree with the Court of Appeals that the Law School sufficiently considered workable race-neutral alternatives. The District Court took the Law School to task for failing to consider race-neutral alternatives such as "using a lottery system" or "decreasing the emphasis for all applicants on undergraduate GPA and LSAT scores." But these alternatives would require a dramatic sacrifice of diversity, the academic quality of all admitted students, or both.

The Law School's current admissions program considers race as one factor among many, in an effort to assemble a student body that is diverse in ways broader than race. Because a lottery would make that kind of nuanced judgment impossible, it would effectively sacrifice all other educational values, not to mention every other kind of diversity. So too with the suggestion that the Law School simply lower admissions standards for all students, a drastic remedy that would require the Law School to become a much different institution and sacrifice a vital component of its educational mission. . . .

Plan Must Not Harm Other Races

We acknowledge that there are serious problems of justice connected with the idea of preference itself. Narrow tailoring, therefore, requires that a race-conscious admissions program not unduly harm members of any racial group. Even remedial race-based governmental action generally remains subject to continuing oversight to assure that it will work the least harm possible to other innocent persons competing for the benefit. To be narrowly tailored, a race-conscious admissions program must not unduly burden individuals who are not members of the favored racial and ethnic groups.

We are satisfied that the Law School's admissions program does not. Because the Law School considers "all pertinent elements of diversity," it can (and does) select nonminority applicants who have greater potential to enhance student body diversity over underrepresented minority applicants. . . .

We agree that, in the context of its individualized inquiry into the possible diversity contributions of all applicants, the Law School's race-conscious admissions program does not unduly harm nonminority applicants.

Durational Requirement

We are mindful, however, that [a] core purpose of the Fourteenth Amendment was to do away with all governmentally imposed discrimination based on race. Accordingly, race-conscious admissions policies must be limited in time. This requirement reflects that racial classifications, however compelling their goals, are potentially so dangerous that they may be employed no more broadly than the interest demands. Enshrining a permanent justification for racial preferences would offend this fundamental equal protection principle. We see no reason to exempt race-conscious admissions programs from the requirement that all governmental use of race must have a logical end point. The Law School, too, concedes that all race-conscious programs must have reasonable durational limits. . . .

We take the Law School at its word that it would "like nothing better than to find a race-neutral admissions formula" and will terminate its race-conscious admissions program as soon as practicable. It has been 25 years since Justice Powell first approved the use of race to further an interest in student body diversity in the context of public higher education. Since that time, the number of minority applicants with high grades and test scores has indeed increased. We expect that 25 years from now, the use of racial preferences will no longer be necessary to further the interest approved today.

"*I do not believe that the Constitution gives the Law School [University of Michigan Law School] such free rein in the use of race.*"

Dissenting Opinion: The Racial Preferences in College Admissions Must Survive Strict Examination

William H. Rehnquist

William H. Rehnquist, an unwavering conservative, was first appointed to the Court by President Nixon in 1972. He was promoted to chief justice in 1986 by President Reagan. He died in 2005, while still a member of the Supreme Court.

Chief Justice Rehnquist, in his dissenting opinion, contends that the law school's admission program is neither narrowly tailored nor strictly scrutinized. The majority opinion, he states, gives excessive deference to the law school's race-based action simply because it involves higher education. The admissions program fails to treat the different minority groups equally; thus it does not succeed in passing strict scrutiny. In addition, the admissions program cannot survive the test of strict scrutiny since it does not provide a precise time limit for the use of racial preferences. The law school's method of achieving diversity is, in fact, racial balancing and imprecise tailoring of a race-based action. Therefore, he argues, the admissions program is unconstitutional.

William H. Rehnquist, dissenting opinion, *Grutter v. Bollinger*, 539 U.S. 306, 2003.

I agree with the Court that, "in the limited circumstance when drawing racial distinctions is permissible," the government must ensure that its means are narrowly tailored to achieve a compelling state interest. I do not believe, however, that the University of Michigan Law School's (Law School) means are narrowly tailored to the interest it asserts. The Law School claims it must take the steps it does to achieve a "critical mass" of underrepresented minority students. But its actual program bears no relation to this asserted goal. Stripped of its "critical mass" veil, the Law School's program is revealed as a naked effort to achieve racial balancing.

Strict Scrutiny Analysis Fails

As we have explained many times, [a]ny preference based on racial or ethnic criteria must necessarily receive a most searching examination. Our cases establish that, in order to withstand this demanding inquiry, respondents must demonstrate that their methods of using race "'fit'" a compelling state interest "with greater precision than any alternative means."

Before the Court's decision today, we consistently applied the same strict scrutiny analysis regardless of the government's purported reason for using race and regardless of the setting in which race was being used. We rejected calls to use more lenient review in the face of claims that race was being used in "good faith" because [m]ore than good motives should be required when government seeks to allocate its resources by way of an explicit racial classification system. We likewise rejected calls to apply more lenient review based on the particular setting in which race is being used. Indeed, even in the specific context of higher education, we emphasized that constitutional limitations protecting individual rights may not be disregarded.

Although the Court recites the language of our strict scrutiny analysis, its application of that review is unprecedented in its deference.

Respondents' asserted justification for the Law School's use of race in the admissions process is obtaining the educational benefits that flow from a diverse student body. They contend that a "critical mass" of underrepresented minorities is necessary to further that interest. Respondents and school administrators explain generally that "critical mass" means a sufficient number of underrepresented minority students to achieve several objectives: To ensure that these minority students do not feel isolated or like spokespersons for their race; to provide adequate opportunities for the type of interaction upon which the educational benefits of diversity depend; and to challenge all students to think critically and reexamine stereotypes. These objectives indicate that "critical mass" relates to the size of the student body.

"Critical Mass" Argument Fails

In practice, the Law School's program bears little or no relation to its asserted goal of achieving "critical mass." Respondents explain that the Law School seeks to accumulate a "critical mass" of *each* underrepresented minority group. But the record demonstrates that the Law School's admissions practices with respect to these groups differ dramatically and cannot be defended under any consistent use of the term "critical mass."

From 1995 through 2000, the Law School admitted between 1,130 and 1,310 students. Of those, between 13 and 19 were Native American, between 91 and 108 were African-Americans, and between 47 and 56 were Hispanic. If the Law School is admitting between 91 and 108 African-Americans in order to achieve "critical mass," thereby preventing African-American students from feeling "isolated or like spokespersons for their race," one would think that a number of the same order of magnitude would be necessary to accomplish the same purpose for Hispanics and Native Americans. Similarly, even if all of the Native American applicants admitted in a given year matriculate, which the record demonstrates is not at all the case, how can this possibly constitute a "critical mass" of Native Americans in a class of over 350 students? In order for this pattern of admission to be consistent with the Law School's explanation of "critical mass," one would have to believe that the objectives of "critical mass" offered by respondents are achieved with only half the number of Hispanics and one-sixth the number of Native Americans as compared to African-Americans. But respondents offer no race-specific reasons for such disparities. Instead, they simply emphasize the importance of achieving "critical mass," without any explanation of why that concept is applied differently among the three underrepresented minority groups.

Respondents have *never* offered any race-specific arguments explaining why significantly more individuals from one underrepresented minority group are needed in order to achieve "critical mass" or further student body diversity. They certainly have not explained why Hispanics, who they have said are among "the groups most isolated by racial barriers in our country," should have their admission capped out in this manner. True, petitioner is neither Hispanic nor Native American. But the Law School's disparate admissions practices with respect to these minority groups demonstrate that its alleged goal of "critical mass" is simply a sham. Petitioner may use these statistics to expose this sham, which is the basis for the Law School's admission of less qualified underrepresented minorities in preference to her. Surely strict scrutiny cannot permit these sort of disparities without at least some explanation.

Racial Balancing Unconstitutional

I do not believe that the Constitution gives the Law School such free rein in the use of race. The Law School has offered no explanation for its actual admissions practices and, unexplained, we are bound to conclude that the Law School has managed its admissions program, not to achieve a "critical mass," but to extend offers of admission to members of selected minority groups in proportion to their statistical representation in the applicant pool. But this is precisely the type of racial balancing that the Court itself calls "patently unconstitutional."

Undetermined Duration Unconstitutional

Finally, I believe that the Law School's program fails strict scrutiny because it is devoid of any reasonably precise time limit on the Law School's use of race in admissions. We have emphasized that we will consider "the planned duration of the remedy" in determining whether a race-conscious program is constitutional. Our previous cases have required some limit on the duration of programs such as this because discrimination on the basis of race is invidious.

The Court suggests a possible 25-year limitation on the Law School's current program. Respondents, on the other hand, remain more ambiguous, explaining that "the Law School of course recognizes that race-conscious programs must have reasonable durational limits, and the Sixth Circuit properly found such a limit in the Law School's resolve to cease considering race when genuine race-neutral alternatives become available." These discussions of a time limit are the vaguest of assurances. In truth, they permit the Law School's use of racial preferences on a seemingly permanent basis. Thus, an important component of strict scrutiny—that a program be limited in time—is casually subverted.

The Court, in an unprecedented display of deference under our strict scrutiny analysis, upholds the Law School's program despite its obvious flaws. We have said that when it comes to the use of race, the connection between the ends and the means used to attain them must be precise. But here the flaw is deeper than that; it is not merely a question of "fit" between ends and means. Here the means actually used are forbidden by the Equal Protection Clause of the Constitution.

> "Preferment by race, when resorted to by the State, can be the most divisive of all policies, containing within it the potential to destroy confidence in the Constitution and in the idea of equality."

Dissenting Opinion: Judicial Review Is Required for Racial Preferences

Anthony M. Kennedy

Anthony M. Kennedy, an experienced federal judge, was appointed to the Supreme Court in 1988 by President Reagan.

Justice Kennedy, in his dissenting opinion, concedes that previous Supreme Court decisions support a university's call for diversity. However, he specifies that the use of racial preference must still face the test of exacting judicial examination, which the University of Michigan Law School fails. The law school's admissions program does not ensure that each applicant receives individual attention. Also, the school's racial preference policy fails short of proving that race is not the predominant consideration in the admission process. Kennedy claims that race-neutral alternatives, which avoid quotas, should have been explored more fully in the majority decision. In general, he believes that the majority decision does not reflect strict scrutiny, especially in its failure to insist that a system based on racial preference be precisely limited in duration.

Anthony M. Kennedy, dissenting opinion, *Grutter v. Bollinger*, 539 U.S. 306, 2003.

The separate opinion by Justice Powell in *Regents of Univ. of Cal. v. Bakke* is based on the principle that a university admissions program may take account of race as one, nonpredominant factor in a system designed to consider each applicant as an individual, provided the program can meet the test of strict scrutiny by the judiciary. This is a unitary formulation. If strict scrutiny is abandoned or manipulated to distort its real and accepted meaning, the Court lacks authority to approve the use of race even in this modest, limited way. The opinion by Justice Powell, in my view, states the correct rule for resolving this case. The Court, however, does not apply strict scrutiny. By trying to say otherwise, it undermines both the test and its own controlling precedents.

Justice Powell's approval of the use of race in university admissions reflected a tradition, grounded in the First Amendment, of acknowledging a university's conception of its educational mission. Our precedents provide a basis for the Court's acceptance of a university's considered judgment that racial diversity among students can further its educational task, when supported by empirical evidence.

Strict Scrutiny Not Applied

It is unfortunate, however, that the Court takes the first part of Justice Powell's rule but abandons the second. Having approved the use of race as a factor in the admissions process, the majority proceeds to nullify the essential safeguard Justice Powell insisted upon as the precondition of the approval. The safeguard was rigorous judicial review, with strict scrutiny as the controlling standard. This Court has reaffirmed, subsequent to *Bakke*, the absolute necessity of strict scrutiny when the states uses race as an operative category. The Court confuses deference to a university's definition of its educational objective with deference to the implementation of this goal. In the context of university admissions the objective of racial diversity can be accepted based on empirical data known to us, but deference is not to be given with respect to the methods by which it is pursued. Preferment by race, when resorted to by the State, can be the most divisive of all policies, containing within it the potential to destroy confidence in the Constitution and in the idea of equality. The majority today refuses to be faithful to the settled principle of strict review designed to reflect these concerns.

Excessive Deference Shown

The Court, in a review that is nothing short of perfunctory, accepts the University of Michigan Law School's assurances that its admissions process meets with constitutional requirements. The majority fails to confront the reality of how the Law School's admissions policy is implemented. The dissenting opinion by The Chief Justice, which I join in full, demonstrates beyond question why the concept of critical mass is a delusion used by the Law School to mask its attempt to make race an automatic factor in most instances and to achieve numerical goals indistinguishable from quotas. An effort to achieve racial balance among the minorities the school seeks to attract is, by the Court's own admission, "patently unconstitutional."

About 80 to 85 percent of the places in the entering class are given to applicants in the upper range of Law School Admissions Test scores and grades. An applicant with these credentials likely will be admitted without consideration of race or ethnicity. With respect to the remaining 15 to 20 percent of the seats, race is likely outcome determinative for many members of minority groups. That is where the competition becomes tight and where any given applicant's chance of admission is far smaller if he or she lacks minority status. At this point the numerical concept of critical mass has the real potential to compromise individual review.

The Law School has not demonstrated how individual consideration is, or can be, preserved at this stage of the application process given the instruction to attain what it calls critical mass. In fact the evidence shows otherwise. . . .

Individual Review Required

The Law School has the burden of proving, in conformance with the standard of strict scrutiny, that it did not utilize race in an unconstitutional way. At the very least, the constancy of admitted minority students and the close correlation between the racial breakdown of admitted minorities and the composition of the applicant pool require the Law School either to produce a convincing explanation or to show it has taken adequate steps to ensure individual assessment. The Law School does neither. . . .

The consultation of daily reports during the last stages in the admissions process suggests there was no further attempt at individual review save for race itself. The admissions officers could use the reports to recalibrate the plus factor given to race depending on how close they were to achieving the Law School's goal of critical mass. The bonus factor of race would then become divorced from individual review; it would be premised instead on the numerical objective set by the Law School.

The Law School made no effort to guard against this danger. It provided no guidelines to its admissions personnel on how to reconcile individual assessment with the directive to admit a critical mass of minority students. The admissions program could have been structured to eliminate at least some of the risk that the promise of individual evaluation was not being kept. The daily consideration of racial breakdown of admitted students is not a feature of affirmative-action programs used by other institutions of higher learning. . . .

Diversity Must Be Achieved
Without Individual Infringement

To be constitutional, a university's compelling interest in a diverse student body must be achieved by a system where individual assessment is safeguarded through the entire process. There is no constitutional objection to the goal of considering race as one modest factor among many others to achieve diversity, but an educational institution must ensure, through sufficient procedures, that each applicant receives individual consideration and that race does not become a predominant factor in the admissions decisionmaking. The Law School failed to comply with this requirement, and by no means has it carried its burden to show otherwise by the test of strict scrutiny. . . .

It is difficult to assess the Court's pronouncement that race-conscious admissions programs will be unnecessary 25 years from now. If it is intended to mitigate the damage the Court does to the concept of strict scrutiny, neither petitioners nor other rejected law school applicants will find solace in knowing the basic protection put in place by Justice Powell will be suspended for a full quarter of a century. Deference is antithetical to strict scrutiny, not consistent with it.

Race-Neutral Alternatives Must Be Explored

As to the interpretation that the opinion contains its own self-destruct mechanism, the majority's abandonment of strict scrutiny undermines this objective. Were the courts to apply a searching standard to race-based admissions schemes, that would force educational institutions to seriously explore race-neutral alternatives. The Court, by contrast, is willing to be satisfied by the Law School's profession of its own good faith. The majority admits as much: "We take the Law School at its word that it would 'like nothing better than to find a race-neutral admissions formula' and will terminate its race-conscious admissions program as soon as practicable."

If universities are given the latitude to administer programs that are tantamount to quotas, they will have few incentives to make the existing minority admissions schemes transparent and protective of individual review. The unhappy consequence will be to perpetuate the hostilities that proper consideration of race is designed to avoid. The perpetuation, of course, would be the worst of all outcomes. Other programs do exist which will be more effective in bringing about the harmony and mutual respect among all citizens that our constitutional tradition has always sought. They, and not the program under review here, should be the model, even if the Court defaults by not demanding it.

Diversity Goal Cannot Suspend Strict Scrutiny

It is regrettable the Court's important holding allowing racial minorities to have their special circumstances considered in order to improve their educational opportunities is accompanied by a suspension of the strict scrutiny which was the predicate of allowing race to be considered in the first place. If the Court abdicates its constitutional duty to give strict scrutiny to the use of race in university admissions, it negates my authority to approve the use of race in pursuit of student diversity. The Constitution cannot confer the right to classify on the basis of race even in this special context absent searching judicial review. For these reasons, though I reiterate my approval of giving appropriate consideration to race in this one context, I must dissent in the present case.

"The landmark decision was an endorsement of the importance of a diverse student body."

More Colleges Are Making Diversity an Important Goal

Tim Grant

Tim Grant is a staff reporter for the Pittsburgh Post-Gazette.

In the following selection, Grant reports that prospective undergraduate students are pondering whether to divulge their race on college applications. Although some colleges and universities accept all applicants, more selective colleges must choose whether to consider race, religion, and gender in admission decisions. In Grutter, *the Supreme Court ruled that race may be considered as one of several factors in admission, though quotas are prohibited.*

Before checking the box to identify her race on her college admissions application, Cecilia Vaughn hesitated for a moment, torn by conflicting emotions.

It was an optional but important question that might increase her chances of being admitted if for no other reason than the fact she is black. Yet she believed her application was strong enough to stand on its own.

She decided to answer the question.

"I'm selling myself, and I want them to know as much about me as possible," said Ms. Vaughn, now a senior at Duquesne University. "I don't want anything to be a surprise."

Efforts to Add Diversity

As more colleges and universities make greater efforts to add diversity to largely white campuses, some admissions officers are considering an applicant's race along with grades and SAT scores.

Affirmative action in the college admissions process has for many years been an issue of national debate. Lawsuits have been filed because of it, and the U.S. Supreme Court has ruled on it, saying that a student's race is one factor that can be used in deciding admissions, but that no quotas are allowed.

"We don't set targets for race, religion or gender. But it is part of our strategic plan to increase diversity on campus," said Paul-James Cukanna, executive director of admissions at Duquesne University.

He said 8 percent of the 1,326 freshmen admitted last fall were from minority groups.

"The vast majority of our minority applicants have test scores, high school records and teacher recommendations that show they have the academic ability to be successful at Duquesne," Mr. Cukanna said. "We're not concerned with the quality of minority applicants. We need more of them. That's why it's nice to know what the race of the applicant is."

Ms. Vaughn, 21, who attended high school in Cleveland, said she was turned off by a recruiter from one college who aggressively pursued her, saying that school wanted to boost minority enrollment.

"I felt it was almost desperate on their part, and I was not in the mood to be a trailblazer," Ms. Vaughn said.

"It was just so weird. They were calling my house, talking to my mom, and I felt if they had to sell to me so hard, it wasn't worth my time to go down there."

The James Irvine Foundation, a California group that seeks to expand opportunities and diversity, recently completed a study of three California colleges that found that a sizable portion of students who chose not to indicate their race in the admissions process were white.

The study noted that the percentage of students in the "unknown" category nearly doubled between 1991 and 2001, from 3.2 percent to 5.9 percent, and on individual campuses the percentage can be much higher.

Support for Color-blind Policies

Roger Clegg, president of the Center for Equal Opportunity in Washington, D.C., which supports color-blind policies, said his organization believes that it is unfair, divisive and often illegal for colleges and universities to give preference on the basis of race in their admissions process.

"We have no objection to racial and ethnic diversity, of course. But we don't think it justifies something as divisive and unfair as discrimination," Mr. Clegg said.

He said his organization had filed complaints with the U.S. Department of Education against North Carolina State University and the College of William & Mary.

"We found substantial evidence that race and ethnicity were being illegally weighted in admissions at those colleges," Mr. Clegg said.

The North Carolina State case is still under investigation, according to David Thomas, spokesman for the U.S. Department of Education. The William & Mary case was closed because there wasn't enough detail for the Office of Civil Rights to act on it. Mr. Clegg's organization appealed, and the appeal is still under review. Many colleges don't refuse any qualified applicants.

Thomas J. Kane, who teaches public policy at Harvard University's John F. Kennedy School of Government, conducted a study that showed that about 60 percent of America's institutions of higher learning admit nearly all who apply and therefore don't give preference to any particular race.

The most competitive colleges fight over the 300 or so African-Americans with the highest grades and SAT scores, he said.

In a major victory for the University of Michigan in June 2003, the U.S. Supreme Court [in *Grutter v. Bollinger*], upheld the right of universities to consider race in college admissions procedures to achieve a diverse student body.

The Right of Preferential Treatment

The landmark decision was an endorsement of the importance of a diverse student body.

"Race and ethnicity is one of a myriad of factors the admissions committee would consider," said Betsy Porter, director of admissions and financial aid at the University of Pittsburgh. "A student would have to be academically admissible in order to be admitted."

But at a school such as Pitt, where there is no SAT cutoff and no minimum standard that applies to every student, it's harder to say who does or does not meet the qualifications.

Dr. Porter said that what matters in getting admitted to Pitt's main campus is class rank, academic grades, SAT scores, extracurricular activities and course work. The school is keenly interested in high school students taking more advanced and honors courses.

"There could be a situation where a student indicates [he or she is] a minority enrolled in a large, urban high school, [has] taken the right mix of courses including AP and honors courses, and [has] done well, but has a relatively low SAT score," she said.

"If [the student] indicated [he or she] worked part time to contribute to the family and has two or three letters of glowing recommendations from clergy or teachers, that would be a student the committee would determine could both benefit from and make a contribution to the college."

About 30 percent of the 4,000 students in this year's entering freshman class at Temple University were African-Americans, Latinos and Asians.

Recruiters there make a point of attending African-American events and high school fairs to reach talented minorities. They also send direct mail and conduct telephone campaigns.

"What we're known for is diversity in our student body, and we're proud of that," said Timm Rinehart, Temple's director of admissions.

Mr. Rinehart said Temple admitted 6 percent more African-Americans this school year than last year, 17 percent more Latinos and 11 percent more Asians, many of whom are immigrants.

"We do practice affirmative action in the applicant decision-making process, not in a narrow quantitative sense, but in a larger holistic perspective. We ask for ethnicity on the application, and as we make a decision, we consider it as one of the subjective factors."

Choosing Diversity

Annie Cunningham, 18, of Braddock, decided to attend a historically black college, Hampton University.

After four years at Shady Side Academy and spending most of her grade-school years in private schools, Ms. Cunningham wanted to get a different point of view through her college experience.

"I'm not used to being in a school environment where everyone is black, where everyone has the same goals and motives," said Ms. Cunningham, a freshman. "I feel it is a positive experience for me because Hampton has a good reputation for being a top school."

She also checked the box on her admissions application concerning her race, although she didn't feel it was necessary because of her high grades and test scores.

In her case, she thinks it's more advantageous for the small number of white students who apply to Hampton to indicate their race.

A Hampton University official, however, said the institution had a race-blind admissions process.

If Hampton were more diverse, Ms. Cunningham said, "I wouldn't get the same thing out of it. It would be the same as going to Shady Side or any other private school."

> "The cold reality is that affirmative action is simply not as powerful—in either a negative or a positive sense—as many people assumed."

Affirmative Action Turns Equality Upside Down

Ellis Cose

Ellis Cose is an author, columnist, and contributing editor for Newsweek. He is also a commentator for public radio and a popular campus lecturer and public speaker.

Even though the Supreme Court has ruled that preferential treatment is an acceptable consideration in college admission, the debate continues. In the pursuit of social justice, affirmative action requires that some groups be treated differently. In the following selection, Cose suggests that the question should not be whether to permit affirmative action, but rather how to vanquish social injustice and provide opportunities to all who deserve it.

State Proposals Banning Affirmative Action

A ffirmative action may not be the most divisive issue on the ballot, but it remains an unending source of conflict and debate—at least in Michigan, whose citizens are pondering a proposal that would ban affirmative action in the public sector. No one knows whether other states will follow

Ellis Cose, "The Color of Change," *Newsweek*, vol. 148, no. 18, November 13, 2006, pp. 52–53. Copyright © 2006 Newsweek, Inc. All rights reserved. Reproduced by permission.

Michigan's lead, but partisans on both sides see the vote as crucial—a decision that could either help or hinder a movement aimed at ending "preferential treatment" programs once and for all.

Ward Connerly has no doubts about the outcome. "There may be some ups and downs ... with regard to [affirmative action], but it's ending," says Connerly, the main mover behind the Michigan proposal, who pushed almost identical propositions to passage in California 10 years ago and in Washington state two years later. His adversaries are equally passionate. "I just want to shout from the rooftops, 'This isn't good for America,'" says Mary Sue Coleman, president of the University of Michigan. She sees no need for Michigan to adopt the measure. "We have a living experiment in California, and it has failed," says Coleman.

Wade Henderson, executive director of the Leadership Conference on Civil Rights, sees something deeply symbolic in the battle. Michigan, in his eyes, is where resegregation began—with a 1974 U.S. Supreme Court decision that tossed out a plan to bus Detroit children to the suburbs. Henderson sees that decision as a prelude to the hypersegregation that now defines much of Michigan. The Supreme Court is currently considering two new cases that could lead to another ruling on how far public school systems can go in their quest to maintain racial balance.

Why Does the Debate Continue?

All of which raises a question: why are we still wrestling with this stuff? Why, more than a quarter of a century after the high court ruled race had a legitimate place in university admissions decisions, are we still fighting over whether race should play a role? Why are we still debating whether programs that attempt to address America's history of discrimination against women and minorities belong in the public sphere?

One answer is that the very idea of affirmative action—that is, systematically treating members of various groups differently in the pursuit of diversity or social justice—strikes some people as downright immoral. For to believe in affirmative action is to believe in a concept of equality turned upside down. It is to believe that "to treat some persons equally, we must treat them differently," as the idea was expressed by U.S. Supreme Court Justice Harry Blackmun.

That argument has never been an easy sell, even when made passionately by President Lyndon B. Johnson during an era in which prejudice was thicker than L.A. smog. Now the argument is infinitely more difficult to make. Even those generally supportive of affirmative action don't like the connotations it sometimes carries. "No one wants preferential treatment, including African-Americans," observed Ed Sarpolis, vice president of EPIC-MRA, a Michigan polling firm.

In 2003, the Supreme Court upheld the University of Michigan's right to use race in the pursuit of "diversity," [*Grutter v. Bollinger*] even as it condemned the way the undergraduate school had chosen to do so. The decision left Jennifer Gratz, the named plaintiff, fuming. "I called Ward Connerly . . . and I said, 'We need to do something about this,'" recalled Gratz, an animated former cheerleader. They decided that if the Supreme Court wouldn't give them what they wanted, they would take their case—and their proposition—directly to the people.

Californians disagree about the impact of Connerly's proposition on their state. But despite some exceedingly grim predictions, the sky did not fall in. Most people went about their lives much as they always had.

California Affected by Public Sector Ban

This is not to say Proposition 209 had no effect. In two areas—minority enrollment in the state's top public universities and contracts awarded to women and minorities—the vote was a watershed event. In 1998, the University of California, Berkeley, admitted less than half the number of blacks it had the previous year and nearly half the number of Latinos. At UCLA, the numbers of incoming "underrepresented" minorities also dropped precipitously. At the law schools, the falloff was startling. In 1997, Berkeley's law school enrolled only one black first-year student out of a total of 268. UCLA did not fare much better.

This summer, UCLA projected its lowest black enrollment (96 prospective students out of nearly 5,000 freshmen) in more than three decades. Partly in response, UCLA's academic senate approved a "holistic" admissions process, meaning the university would focus on the whole student—not just the academics—and hope for a more diverse student body.

The impact of Proposition 209 on small entrepreneurs was even more striking. In the preproposition years, it was easy to find minority firms to work on major transportation projects, said Frederick Jordan, founder of F.E. Jordan Associates, a civil and environmental engineering firm. But "all the firms were wiped out. In 1996 in San Francisco I could've produced 10 or 15 African-American firms that could do any kind of work. Today, I can't find anybody—zero, zero." A study released by the Discrimination Research Center confirms that only a third of minority enterprises certified to do business with the California Department of Transportation in 1996 are still in operation.

Before the proposition passed, its proponents were fond of arguing that minority students would be happier since they would finally be free of the "stigma" associated with affirmative action. Kimberly Griffin, a black UCLA graduate student, says they were wrong: "People on campus . . . think there's still affirmative action and there are still quotas. So they're like, 'How could there be so many black or brown people here if there's no affirmative action?'"

It is also far from clear, as proponents of Proposition 209 insisted would be the case, that barring consideration of race results in a better match between university and student. Or that it improved graduation rates, since students who got into school on the basis of "merit," as opposed to affirmative action supposedly would be more likely to succeed. On those questions the evidence, at best, seems mixed.

Affirmative Action Lacks Force

Despite the California experience, few people involved in the early debates seem much interested in revising their old assumptions. The cold reality is that affirmative action is simply not as powerful—in either a negative or a positive sense—as many people assumed.

Affirmative Action was never meant to carry the weight society threw on its shoulders. It was never supposed to rescue the poor, enlighten the illiterate or feed the hungry. It was not meant to make up for the inadequacies of a bad K-12 education. It was a modest attempt to give a bit of a boost to a handful of folks from a race of people who had been unfairly held back for centuries. But because the nation lacked the will or knowledge to solve the big problems, we charged affirmative action with doing it all. So though the public often saw it as a powerful force, ruthlessly crushing white male aspirations and elevating hordes of minorities and women, its actual impact was rather small (albeit crucial in certain areas).

Will Affirmative Action Survive Long Enough to Right Social Wrongs?

The choice America faces is not about ending affirmative action—at some point, as both its critics and defenders agree, the affirmative-action tugboat will run out of steam. The question is whether, before that happens, society will find the will and resources to vanquish the problems that gave rise to it in the first place. No child chooses to be born into poverty with parents who are semiliterate or to live in neighborhoods where the schools are little more than holding pens. The cause of early-childhood education would seem a natural for the proponents of anti-affirmative action initiatives. Yet, for the most part, they seem uninterested in that fight which, if successful, really could render affirmative action irrelevant.

In a sane world, the battle in Michigan, and indeed the battle over affirmative action *writ large*, would offer an opportunity to seriously engage a question the enemies and defenders of affirmative action claim to care about: how do you go about creating a society where all people—not just the lucky few—have the opportunities they deserve? It is a question much broader than the debate over affirmative action. But until we begin to move toward an answer, the debate over affirmative action will continue—even if it is something of a sideshow to what should be the main event.

Organizations to Contact

The editors have compiled the following list of organizations concerned with the issues debated in this book. The descriptions are derived from materials provided by the organizations. All have publications or information available for interested readers. The list was compiled on the date of publication of the present volume; the information provided here may change. Be aware that many organizations take several weeks or longer to respond to inquiries, so allow as much time as possible.

American Civil Liberties Union (ACLU)
125 Broad Street, 17th Floor, New York, NY   10004
(212) 607-3300 • fax: (212) 607-3318
Web site: www.aclu.org

The mission of the ACLU is to preserve the protections and guarantees of the Bill of Rights, other amendments, and other rights providing equal protection and equal treatment under the law—including affirmative action. The ACLU handles nearly 6,000 court cases annually, actively tracks courts and legislatures, and issues a series of *ACLU Briefing Reports* on every major civil-rights topic.

Canadian Human Rights Commission (CHRC)
344 Slater Street, 8th Floor, Ottawa, ON   K1A 1E1
  CANADA
(613) 995-1151 • fax: (613) 996-9661
e-mail: info.com@chrc-ccdp.ca
Web site: http://www.chrc-ccdp.ca

Established in 1978, the Canadian Human Rights Commission educates Canadians on human rights issues, provides effective and timely means for resolving individual complaints, and helps reduce barriers to equality in employment and access to services.

Center for Equal Opportunity (CEO)
7700 Leesburg Pike, Suite 231, Falls Church, VA   22043
(703) 442-0066 • fax: (703) 442-0449
Web site: www.ceousa.org

The Center for Equal Opportunity promotes color-blind equal-opportunity policies while seeking to halt the expansion of racial preferences in employment, education, and voting. CEO testifies before federal and state agencies, files amicus briefs with the Supreme Court, drafts federal and state legislation, and issues reports on racial public policies. Recent publications include: *Racial and Ethnic Preferences and Consequences at the University of Maryland School of Medicine*, and *Pervasive Preferences: Racial and Ethnic Discrimination in Undergraduate Admissions across the Nation.*

The Claremont Institute
937 West Foothill Boulevard, Suite E, Claremont, CA   91711
(909) 621-6825 • fax: (909) 626-8724
e-mail: info@claremont.org
Web site: http://www.claremont.org

The Claremont Institute supports limited government and opposes affirmative action initiatives. Its publications include *America's Passion for Fairness, The Affirmative Action Trainwreck: Why "Mend It, Don't End It" Won't Work,* and *Equal Opportunity Denied: Nine Case Studies in Reverse Discrimination.*

Coalition to Defend Affirmative Action, Integration & Immigrant Rights and Fight for Equality by Any Means Necessary (BAMN)
P.O. Box 24834, Detroit, MI   48224
(313) 438-3748
e-mail: letters@bamn.com
Web site: www.bamn.com

BAMN is a national organization dedicated to establishing a new civil-rights movement to defend affirmative action, integration, and other gains of the early civil-rights movement. Activities include organizing chapters, filing lawsuits, circulating petitions, issuing press releases, and publishing the *Liberator*.

The Heritage Foundation
214 Massachusetts Ave. NE, Washington, DC   20002-4999
(202) 546-4400 • fax: (202) 544-8328
e-mail: info@heritage.org
Web site: http://www.heritage.org

The foundation is a conservative public policy research institute dedicated to free-market principles, individual liberty, and limited government. It opposes affirmative action for women and minorities and believes the private sector, not government, should be relied upon to ease social problems and to improve the status of women and minorities. The foundation publishes the periodic *Backgrounder* and the quarterly *Policy Review* as well as numerous monographs, books, and papers on public policy issues.

Leadership Conference on Civil Rights (LCCR)
1629 K Street NW, 10th Floor, Washington, DC   20006
(202) 466-3311
Web site: www.civilrights.org

Founded in 1950, the LCCR is the premier civil-rights coalition, orchestrating the national legislative campaign on behalf of every major civil-rights law since 1957. The LCCR provides relevant and breaking news and information on civil-rights concerns, including affirmative action. The coalition publishes e-mail newsletters, reports, curricula, and a quarterly publication, the *Civil Rights Monitor*.

National Association for the Advancement of Colored People (NAACP)
4805 Mt. Hope Drive, Baltimore, MD   21215
(877) NAACP-98
Web site: http://www.naacp.org

The NAACP is the oldest and largest civil rights organization in the United States. Its principal objectives are to achieve equal rights and to eliminate racial prejudice by removing racial discrimination in housing, employment, voting, education, the courts, and business. The NAACP publishes a variety of newsletters, books, and pamphlets as well as the magazine *Crisis.*

National Center for Public Policy Research
501 Capitol Court NE, Washington, DC   20002
(202) 543-4110 • fax: (202) 543-5975
e-mail: info@nationalcenter.org
Web site: www.nationalcenter.org

Through the National Leadership Network of Black Conservatives, the National Center for Public Policy Research created Project 21, a coalition of moderate and conservative African American activists. Project 21 actively promotes the viewpoints of the organization and educates the public and Congress on ways to reduce government spending and embrace greater community involvement. Project 21 has published a book of essays, *Black America 1994: Changing Direction*, major reports including *The Health Care Ghetto: African-Americans and Health Care Reform*, and a study in 2002 titled *Smart Growth and Its Effects on Housing Markets: The New Segregation.*

National Organization for Women (NOW)
1100 H Street NW, 3rd Floor, Washington, DC   20005
(202) 628-8669 • fax (202) 785-8576
email: now@now.org
Web site: www.now.org

NOW promotes affirmative action and stresses that women and people of color still face discrimination, despite gains made by civil-rights and women's-rights movements. NOW's goal is to establish equality for all women by working to eliminate discrimination. Activities include: creating legal clinics, forming meetings and rallies, filing petitions, issuing press releases, and lobbying legislators. NOW publishes the *National NOW Times.*

U.S. Equal Employment Opportunity Commission (EEOC)
1801 L Street NW, Washington, DC   20507
(202) 663-4900
Web site: http://www.eeoc.gov

The mission of the EEOC is to promote equal opportunity in employment through administrative and judicial enforcement of the federal civil rights laws and through education and technical assistance. It publishes numerous press releases pertaining to affirmative action.

For Further Research

Books

Terry H. Anderson, *The Pursuit of Fairness: A History of Affirmative Action*. New York: Oxford University Press, 2004.

James A. Beckman, ed., *Affirmative Action: An Encyclopedia*. Westport, CT: Greenwood Publishing Group, 2004.

Eduardo Bonilla-Silva, *Racism without Racists: Color-Blind Racism and the Persistence of Racial Inequality*. New York: Rowman & Littlefield, 2003.

William G. Bowen and Derek Bok, *The Shape of the River: Long-Term Consequences of Considering Race in College and University Admissions*. Princeton, NJ: Princeton University Press, 1998.

Michael K. Brown, et al., *White-Washing Race: The Myth of a Color-Blind Society*. Berkeley: University of California Press, 2003.

Lee Corkorinos, *The Assault on Diversity: An Organized Challenge to Racial and Gender Justice*. Lanham, MD: Rowman & Littlefield, 2003.

Hugh Davis Graham, *Collision Course: The Strange Convergence of Affirmative Action and Immigration Policy*. New York: Oxford University Press, 2002.

Terry Eastland, *Ending Affirmative Action: The Case for Colorblind Justice*. New York: Basic Books, 1996.

Christopher Edley Jr., *Not All Black and White: Affirmative Action and American Values*. New York: Hill & Wang, 1996.

Richard Epstein, *Forbidden Grounds: The Case against Employment Discrimination Laws*. Cambridge, MA: Harvard University Press, 1992.

Robert A. Ibarra, *Beyond Affirmative Action: Reframing the Context of Higher Education*. Madison: University of Wisconsin Press, 2001.

Lesley A. Jacobs, *Pursuing Equal Opportunities: The Theory and Practice of Egalitarian Justice*. Cambridge, England: Cambridge University Press, 2004.

Ira Katznelson, *When Affirmative Action Was White: An Untold History of Racial Inequality in Twentieth-Century America*. New York: Norton & Company, Inc., 2005.

Bob Laird, *The Case for Affirmative Action in University Admissions*. Richmond, CA: Bay Tree, 2005.

Lex K. Larson, *Employment Discrimination*. Newark, NJ: Matthew Bender & Company, 2⁰ ed., 2003.

Stephen Grant Meyer, *As Long as They Don't Move Next Door: Segregation and Racial Conflict in American Neighborhoods*. New York: Rowman & Littlefield, 2000.

Gary Orfield with Michael Kurlaender, eds., *Diversity Challenged: Evidence on the Impact of Affirmative Action*. Cambridge, MA: Harvard Education Publishing Group, 2001.

Greg Stohr, *A Black and White Case: How Affirmative Action Survived Its Greatest Legal Challenge*. Princeton, NJ: Bloomberg Press, 2004.

Periodicals

Elizabeth S. Anderson, "Integration, Affirmative Action, and Strict Scrutiny," *New York University Law Review*, vol. 77, November 2002.

Michelle Wilde Anderson, "Colorblind Segregation: Equal Protection as a Bar to Neighborhood Integration," *California Law Review*, vol. 92, no. 3, May 2004.

Derrick Bell, "Diversity's Distractions," *Columbia Law Review*, vol. 103, 2003.

Francine D. Blau and Anne E. Winkler, "Does Affirmative Action Work?" *Federal Reserve Bank Boston Regional Review*, January 2005.

Michael Boylan, "Affirmative Action: Strategies for the Future," *Journal of Social Philosophy*, vol. 33, no. 1, spring 2002.

Devon W. Carbado and Mitu Gulati, "Race to the Top of the Corporate Ladder: What Minorities Do When They Get There," *Washington & Lee Law Review*, vol. 61, 2004.

Christian Science Monitor, "New Ways to Peace," December 1, 2000.

Chronicle of Higher Education, "Advocates for Black Students Worry that Foes of Affirmative Action Have Found New Avenue of Attack," January 23, 2007.

Chronicle of Higher Education, "Towson U. Gives Men with Low Grades a Chance at College," January 23, 2007.

Kim Clark, "Decision Time," *U.S. News & World Report*, April 19, 2004.

Ward Connelly, "The Michigan Win," *National Review*, January 30, 2007.

Cynthia Estlund, "Working Together: The Workplace, Civil Society, and the Law," *Georgetown Law Review Journal*, vol. 89, no. 1, 2000.

Barbara Fick, "The Case for Maintaining and Encouraging the Use of Voluntary Affirmative Action in Private Sector Employment," *Notre Dame Journal of Law, Ethics & Public Policy*, vol. 11, 1997.

Kim Forde-Mazrui, "Taking Conservatives Seriously: A Moral Justification for Affirmative Action and Reparations," *California Law Review*, vol. 92, 2004.

Paul Frymer and John D. Skrentny, "The Rise of Instrumental Affirmative Action: Law and the New Significance of Race in America," *Connecticut Law Review*, vol. 36, spring 2004.

Robert P. George, "Gratz and Grutter: Some Hard Questions," *Columbia Law Review*, vol. 103, no. 6, 2003.

Dave Gershman, "Minority Students to Face Legal Critique," *Ann Arbor News*, June 22, 2004.

Margaret Gibelman, "Affirmative Action at the Crossroads: A Social Justice Perspective," *Journal of Sociology and Social Welfare*, vol. 27, no. 1, March 2000.

Daniel Golden, "Not Black and White," *Wall Street Journal Classroom Edition*, March 2004.

Lani Guinier and Susan Sturm, "The Future of Affirmative Action," *Boston Review*, December 2000/January 2001.

Mane Hajdin, "Affirmative Action, Old and New," *Journal of Social Philosophy*, vol. 33, no. 1, spring 2002.

D.W. Haslett, "Workplace Discrimination, Good Cause, and Color Blindness," *Journal of Value Inquiry*, vol. 36, no. 1, 2002.

Madeline E. Heilman, "Sex Discrimination and the Affirmative Action Remedy: The Role of Sex Stereotypes," *Journal of Business Ethics*, vol. 16, no. 9, June 1997.

Emmett Hogan, "Affirmative Action Harms Black Colleges," *The Dartmouth Review*, May 7, 2001.

Ira Katznelson, "When Is Affirmative Action Fair? On Grievous Harms and Public Remedies," *Social Research*, vol. 73, no. 2, summer 2006.

Joe Klein, "Can We Improve on Affirmative Action?" *Time*, December 10, 2006.

New York Times, "Colleges Regroup after Voters Ban Race Preferences," January 30, 2007.

Helen Norton, "Stepping through Grutter's Open Doors: What the University of Michigan Affirmative Action Cases Mean for Race-Conscious Government Decision-making," *Temple Law Review*, vol. 78, no. 3, fall 2005.

Daria Roithmayr, "Tacking Left: A Radical Critique of Grutter," *Constitutional Commentary*, vol. 21, 2004.

Charlie Savage, "Robert's Vote Seen as Critical in Racial Issues: Earlier Writings Opposed Affirmative Action Plans," *Boston Globe*, August 7, 2005.

Peter Schmidt, "Affirmative Action Remains a Minefield, Mostly Unmapped," *Chronicle of Higher Education*, October 24, 2003.

Thomas Sowell, "The Grand Fraud: Affirmative Action for Blacks," *Capitalism Magazine*, April 2003.

J.H. Verkerke, "Disaggregating Anti-Discrimination and Accommodation," *William and Mary Law Review*, vol. 44, February 2003.

Roger Wilkins, "Racism Has Its Privileges," *Nation*, March 27, 1995.

Web Sites

Affirmative Action and Diversity Project: A Web Page for Research (http://aad.english.ucsb.edu/). Rather than taking a particular stance on affirmative action, this Web site offers a range of opinions. An academic resource site, it provides numerous articles, policy documents, legislative updates, and an annotated bibliography of research and teaching materials. New links and documents are updated frequently.

Affirmative Action: Playing Favorites (http://www.angel
fire.com/pa/sergeman/issues/affact.html). This Web site
takes a position against affirmative action, stating that
discrimination on the basis of race is detrimental to indi-
vidualism and to companies that seek to hire using affirmative action. The site contains several links to other
sites and references to articles and commentaries against
affirmative action.

Ethnic Majority.com (www.ethnicmajority.com/affirm
ative-action.htm). Founded in 2002, this Web site favors
affirmative action by seeking to educate, assist, and em-
power minorities to achieve advancement in business and
politics. The site features an e-mail newsletter, blogs, job-
search assistance, news links, and references to other related sites and organizations.

Index

D

Davis, Washington v. (1976), 68, 74

Department of Housing and Urban Development, U.S., 81–82

Disabilities, race compared with, 127–129

Diversity
benefits of, 143–144
colleges are making an important goal, 161–166
as legitimate goal of colleges, 141–143
in workplace, variables in, 50–51

Due Process Clause (5th Amendment), 90

Duke Power Co., Griggs v. (1971), 85

E

EEOC, Local 28 of Sheet Metal Workers International Association v. (1986), 129

Equal Credit Opportunity Act (1974), 40

Equal Employment Opportunity Commission (EEOC), 54

Equal Pay Act, 40

Equal Protection Clause (14th Amendment), 14, 15, 18
gender discrimination and, 58
proof of intent to show violation of, 65, 68
race-based affirmative action and, 56–58
in *Reed* decision, 27–28
requires strict scrutiny, 140–141
satisfies strict scrutiny test, 99–100

F

Fair Housing Amendments Act (1988), 84

Family and Medical Leave Act (1993), 44

Fortune 500 companies, women holding directors seats in, 36

Freeman, Lance, 80–81

Fullilove v. Klutznick (1980), 90, 96, 99

G

Gender-based affirmative action, 15
dissimilar treatment based on, is unconstitutional, 39
intermediate vs. strict scrutiny of, 58–59

Gingrich, Newt, 81

Glass Ceiling Act (1991), 43

Glass Ceiling Commission, 43

Gratz v. Bollinger (2003), 57, 58, 61

Griffin, Kimberly, 171

Griggs v. Duke Power Co. (1971), 85

Grutter, Barbara, 134, 139

Grutter v. Bollinger (2003), 16, 17–18, 19, 57–58, 61, 164
case overview, 134–136
decision in, 137–149
dissenting opinion in, 150–154, 155–160

H

Henderson, Wade, 168

Housing Choice Voucher Program, 87